Rossiter Johnson

The Hero of Manila

Dewey on the Mississippi and the Pacific

Rossiter Johnson

The Hero of Manila
Dewey on the Mississippi and the Pacific

ISBN/EAN: 9783743320673

Manufactured in Europe, USA, Canada, Australia, Japa

Cover: Foto ©ninafisch / pixelio.de

Manufactured and distributed by brebook publishing software (www.brebook.com)

Rossiter Johnson

The Hero of Manila

PREFACE.

If this little book does not show for itself why it was written, how it was written, and for whom it was written, not only a preface but the entire text would be useless. The author believes that in every life that is greatly useful to mankind there is a plan and a purpose from the beginning, whether the immediate owner of that life is aware of it or not; and that the art of the biographer—whether he is dealing with facts exclusively or is mingling fact and fiction—should make it discernible by the reader.

The authorities that have been consulted include the Life of David Glasgow Farragut, by his son; Admiral Ammen's Atlantic Coast; Greene's The Mississippi; Battles and Leaders of the Civil War; The Rebellion Record; Marshall's History of the Naval Academy, and especially Adelbert M. Dewey's Life and Letters of Admiral Dewey.

R. J.

Amagansett, *September 8, 1899.*

CONTENTS.

CHAPTER	PAGE
I.—The philosophy of fighting	1
II.—On the river bank	12
III.—Battle royal	23
IV.—Education at Norwich	34
V.—Life at Annapolis	41
VI.—The beginning of war	56
VII.—The fight for New Orleans	68
VIII.—The battle at Port Hudson	92
IX.—The capture of Fort Fisher	105
X.—In time of peace	112
XI.—The battle of Manila	116
XII.—After the battle	130
XIII.—The problem on land	139
XIV.—Honors	145
XV.—Letters	149

LIST OF ILLUSTRATIONS.

	FACING PAGE
Midshipman Dewey	*Frontispiece*
By B. West Clinedinst	
An early battle	10
By B. West Clinedinst	
A schoolroom episode	31
By B. West Clinedinst	
Scene of naval operations in Western rivers	65
Farragut and Dewey	69
By B. West Clinedinst	
Whitewashing the decks	73
By B. West Clinedinst	
Order of attack on Forts Jackson and St. Philip	84
Farragut's fleet passing the forts	89
Order of attack on Port Hudson	95
Passage of the batteries of Port Hudson	98
Removing the wounded	104
By B. West Clinedinst	
Diagram of Manila Bay	116
U. S. Cruiser Olympia, Admiral Dewey's Flagship	122
The battle of Manila	126
Admiral Dewey on the bridge of the Olympia	131
Medal presented by Congress	139
Sword presented by Congress	145
Shield presented to the Olympia	148
Dewey Triumphal Arch, New York	151
Charles R. Lamb, Architect	

The house in which Admiral Dewey was born in Montpelier, Vermont.

THE HERO OF MANILA.

CHAPTER I.

THE PHILOSOPHY OF FIGHTING.

It is not necessary to visit the Bay of Naples in order to witness a beautiful sunset. Our own atmosphere and our own waters produce those that are quite as gorgeous, while our own mountains and woodlands give them as worthy a setting as any in the world.

Half a century ago a little boy sat at his chamber window in Vermont looking at a summer sunset. He was so absorbed in the scene before him and in his own thoughts that he did not notice the entrance of his father until he spoke.

"What are you thinking about, George?" said the father.

"About ships," the boy answered, without turning his head.

"What kind of ships?"

"I can see nearly every kind," said George.

"See them—where?" said his father, looking over his shoulder.

"Right there in the sunset clouds," said the boy.

"Oh!" said his father; and then, after looking a while, added, "Suppose you point out a few of them."

"Do you see that small cloud, at some distance from the others—the one that is rather long and narrow, with a narrower one alongside?"

"Yes, I see that."

"Well, that," said the boy, "is a Brazilian catamaran, and those little knobs at the top are the heads of the men that are paddling it."

"Just so," said his father. "What else can you see?"

"The catamaran," said George, "is pulling out to that clipper ship which has just come to anchor off the port. The clipper is the large one, with her sails furled. Probably the Indians have some fruit on board, which they hope to sell to the sailors."

"Quite natural," said the father.

"And that smaller one, under full sail, fore-and-aft rigged, is a schooner in the coasting trade."

"That one appears to be changing shape rapidly," said the father.

"Yes," said the boy. "She is tacking, and you see her at a different angle."

"I might have suspected as much," said the father, "but I never was a good sailor."

"That very large one," continued the boy, "with a big spread of canvas and holes in her hull, where the red sunlight pours through, is an old-fashioned seventy-four, with all her battle-lanterns lit."

"A pretty fancy," said the father, who evidently was becoming more interested and better able to see the pictures that were so vivid to his son.

"Do you see that dark one over at the right, with one near it that is very red and very ragged?" said the boy.

"I do."

"Those are the Constitution and the Java. They had their famous battle yesterday, and the Java was so badly cut up that to-day Bainbridge has removed her crew and set her on fire. She will blow up pretty soon."

"I should like to see it," said the father.

"And if you look over there to the left," said the boy, "you see quite a collection of rather small ones, most of them very red, some half red and half black. It looks a little confused at first, but when you know what it is you can see plainly enough that it is the battle of Lake Erie. In the very center there is a small boat, and on it something that looks black and blue and red, with a little white. The black is cannon smoke. The blue and red and white is the American flag, which Perry is taking over to the Niagara, because the Lawrence is so badly damaged that he has had to leave her. That one with only one mast standing is the Lawrence."

"Yes, my son, I think you have accounted beautifully for everything there except one. What is that dark one, with rounded ends and no mast, just beyond the clipper?"

"Oh, that," said the boy, taking a moment for reflection, "I think that must be a bullhead boat on the Delaware and Hudson Canal."

"It is a good representation of one," said his father, smiling. "But, George, how came you to know so much about ships and boats and naval history?"

"By reading all I could find about them, sir."

"Well, George, I am really pleased," said Dr. Dewey; "pleased and encouraged to know that you have taken to reading instead of fighting. I was afraid you never would love books; but now that you have begun, you shall have all the good ones you will read."

"Thank you, father, I shall be glad of them."

"But come now, my son, supper is ready, and your sister is waiting for us."

"I will come pretty soon," said George, and his father descended the stairs.

A little later the boy went slowly down, and quietly slipped into his place at the table.

In a few minutes Dr. Dewey looked up, then started as if surprised, and dropped his hands to the edge of the table. He took a sharp look at George, and then said:

"What does that mean? How came you by that black eye?"

"There is only one way to get a black eye that I know of," said the boy.

"Fighting?"

"Yes, sir."

The doctor was silent for several minutes, and then said:

"I don't know what to say to you or do to you, my son. You know what I have said to you about your fighting habit, and you know that I mean it, for I have not only talked to you, but punished you. When I found you had been reading history I took new hope, for I thought you must have got past the fighting age and given your mind to better things. But here you are again with the marks of a pugilist."

"I don't fight when I can help it, and I'm afraid I never shall get past the fighting age," said George.

"Don't fight when you can help it?" said his father. "Can't you always help it?"

"I might by running away. Do you want me to do that?" the boy answered quietly.

"Of course I don't," said the doctor quickly. "But can't you *keep* away?"

"I have to go to school," said George, "and I have to be with the boys; and some of them are quarrelsome, and some are full of conceit, and some need a good licking now and then."

"And you consider it your duty to administer it," said the doctor. "Conceit is a crime that can not be too severely punished."

The boy felt the irony of his father's remark, and saw that he did not quite understand that use of the word "conceit," so he proceeded to explain:

"When a boy goes about bragging how many boys he has licked, and how many others he can lick, and how he will do this, that, and the other thing, if everybody doesn't look out, we say he is too conceited and he ought to have the conceit taken out of him; and the first good chance we get we take it out."

"Suppose you left it in him and paid no attention to it—what would happen in that case?" said the doctor.

"He would grow more and more conceited," said George, "and make himself so disagreeable that the boys couldn't enjoy life, and before a great while you would find him picking on smaller boys than himself and licking them, just to have more brag."

"Do you really have any such boys among your schoolfellows, or is this only theoretical?" the doctor inquired.

"There are a few," said George.

"And how do you determine whose duty it is to take the conceit out of one of them? Do you draw lots, or take turns?"

"The boy that enjoys the job the most generally gets it," said George.

"Just so," said the doctor. "And is there some one boy in the school who enjoys the job, as you call it, more than all the others?"

George evidently felt that this question came so near home he ought not to be expected to answer it, and he was silent.

His elder sister, Mary (they had lost their mother five years before), now spoke for the first time.

"Perhaps," said she, "we ought to ask George to tell us the circumstances of this last fight. I don't believe he is always the one to blame."

"Certainly," said the doctor; "that is only fair. Tell us all about it, George."

Thereupon the boy proceeded to tell them all about it in a very animated manner.

"Bill Ammon," he began, "is one of the bossingest boys in school. He expects to have everything his way. I don't blame a boy for wanting things his own way if he takes fair means to get them so, but Bill doesn't always. You and the teacher tell me that bad habits grow worse and worse, and I suppose it was that way with Bill. At any rate, we found out a few days ago that he was taking regular toll out of two smaller boys—Jimmy Nash and Teddy Hawkins—for not licking them. Each of them had to bring him something twice a week—apples, or nuts, or marbles, or candy, or something else that he wanted—and he threatened not only to lick them if they did not bring the things, but to lick them twice as hard if they told any one about it."

"Why did those boys submit to such treatment?" said the doctor.

"Well, you see," said George, "Jimmy Nash's father is a Quaker, and doesn't believe in hurting anybody, and so if Jimmy gets into any trouble he whales him like fury as soon as he finds it out. And Teddy Hawkins's mother gives him plenty of spending money, so he is always able to buy a little something to please Bill, and I suppose he would rather do that than fight."

"If they were boys of any spirit," said the doctor indignantly, "I should think they would join forces and give Bill the thrashing he deserves. The two together ought to be able to do it."

"Yes, they could," said George; "but, you see, they are not twins, and can't always be together—in fact, they live a long way apart—and as soon as Bill caught either of them alone he would make him pay dear for it. He needed to be licked by some one boy."

"I see," said the doctor; "a Decatur was wanted, to put an end to the tribute."

"Exactly!" said George, and his father's eyes twinkled with pleasure to see that he understood the allusion. He was specially anxious that his boy should become familiar with American history, but he had no anticipation that his son would one day make American history.

"When we found it out," George continued, "Bill tried to make us believe that Jimmy and Teddy were simply paying him to protect them. He said he was their best friend. 'What protection do they need?' said I. 'They are peaceable little fellows, and there is nobody that would be coward enough to attack them.' Bill saw that he was cornered on the argument, and at the same time he got mad at the word coward, thinking I meant it for him. I didn't, for I don't consider him a coward at all."

"Not if he *is* a bully?" said the doctor.

"No, sir," said George. "He certainly is something of a bully, but he is not cowardly."

"There you agree with Charles Lamb," said the doctor.

"Who is Charles Lamb?" said George.

"He was an Englishman, who died fifteen or twenty years ago," said the doctor, "and I hope you'll read his delightful essays some day—but not till you've mastered American history. Attend to that first."

"I'll try to," said George. "When Bill flared up at that word he seemed to lose his head a little. 'Who are you calling a coward?' said he, coming up close to me, with his fist clenched. I said I never called anybody a coward, because if he wasn't one it wouldn't be true, and if he was everybody would find it out soon enough, without my telling them. 'Well, you meant it for me,' said he, 'and you'll have to fight it out, so you'd better take off your jacket mighty quick.' I said I had no objection——"

"You had no objection!" exclaimed his sister Mary.

"Well—that is—under the circumstances," said George, "I didn't see how I could have any. I had

An early battle.

no right to have any. Those two boys did need protection—they needed to be protected against Bill Ammon, who was robbing them. And I thought I might as well do it as anybody. So I said, 'Come over to the orchard, boys,' and we all went. Teddy Hawkins held my jacket, and Sim Nelson held Bill's. We squared off and sparred a little while, and I suppose I must have been careless, for Bill got the first clip at me, landing on my eye. But pretty soon I fetched him a good one under the cheek bone, and followed that up with a smasher on——"

Here Mary turned pale, and showed signs of uneasiness and repugnance. George, who was warming up with his subject, did not notice her, but was going on with his description of the fight, when his father stopped him.

"Your sister," he said, "has no taste for these particulars. Never mind them until some time when you and I are alone. Only tell us how it turned out."

"The boys said it turned out that I gave Bill what he deserved, and I hope I did, but I didn't tell them what a mighty hard job I found it."

"Bravo, George!" exclaimed the doctor, and then quickly added: "But don't fight any more."

CHAPTER II.

ON THE RIVER BANK.

A GROUP of boys sat on the bank of Onion River, looking at the water and occasionally casting pebbles into it. Wet hair, bare feet, and other circumstances indicated that they had not long been out of it. Below them, in one of the comparatively shallow, flat-bottomed reaches, a company of smaller boys were paddling about, some taking their first lessons in swimming, some struggling to duck each other, and some carefully keeping aloof for fear of being ducked. Trees, rocks, broken sunlight, and a summer breeze made the little scene quite Arcadian.

"My uncle is going to California to dig gold," said one of the larger boys, who answered to the name of Tom Kennedy.

"My father says they have discovered gold mines in Australia that are richer than those in California," said another, Felix Ostrom by name.

"But that is twice as far away," said the first speaker, "and you can only get there by a long sea voyage. You can go overland to California, and be in our own country all the time. Isn't that a great deal better, even if you don't get quite so much gold?"

"It wouldn't be better for me," answered George Dewey. "I would rather go by sea, and would rather go to other countries. I want to see as many of them as I can. I would especially like to sail in the Pacific Ocean."

"Why the Pacific?" said Tom.

"Because," said George, "that is not only the largest ocean in the world, but it has the most islands and touches the countries that we know the least about."

"It's an ugly thing to get to it, round Cape Horn," said Felix.

"You can go through the Strait of Magellan," said George. "Last week I found a book of voyages in my Aunt Lavinia's house, and I've been reading all about Magellan. He was the discoverer of the Pacific Ocean, and he sailed through that strait to find it."

"He must have been a very modest man," said Tom.

"Why?"

"Because he didn't name it Magellan Ocean."

"He called it the Pacific because he found it so calm," said George. "And he sailed clear across it. Just think of coming to an unknown sea five or six thousand miles wide, and sailing right out into it, and on and on, past islands and reefs, and sometimes long stretches with nothing in sight but sky and water, and no way to tell when you'll come to the end of it! And when you stop at an island you don't know what you'll find, or whether you'll find anything— even good drinking-water. And he didn't know whether the earth was really round, for no one had ever sailed round it before. I think that beats Columbus."

"Was he really the first one to sail round the world?" said Felix.

"Not exactly," said George. "His ship was the first that ever went round, but he didn't get round with her."

"Why not?"

"Because when they got to the Philippine Islands, which they discovered, they went ashore on one of them and had a fight with the natives, and Magellan was killed."

"I guess the Philippine Islands are pretty good ones to keep away from," said Sammy Atkinson.

"I should be willing to take my chances, if I could get there," said George. "But I suppose I never shall."

"You can't tell," said Sandy Miller, a boy who had recently come from Scotland with his parents, "what savage countries you may visit afore you die. Two years ago I didn't dream I'd ever come to America."

"Do you call ours a savage country?" said Felix, with a twinkle in his eye.

"I didn't exactly mean to," said Sandy, "and yet I think I might, when I remember how all you boys wanted to fight me the first week I was here, only because I was a stranger."

"Not quite all," said George.

"No, I take that back," said Sandy. "You say truly not quite all, for you yourself didn't, and I mustn't forget it of you. I suppose it's human nature to want to fight all strangers, and maybe that's the reason the Philippine men killed Master Magellan. I suppose they'd try to do the same if anybody went there now. But I wish you'd tell us more about him and about the Pacific and the Philippines, for I am aye fond of the sea; I enjoyed every wave on the Atlantic when we came over."

Thereupon George, being urged by the other boys as well, gave an account, as nearly as he could remember, of what he had read.

"What has become of those islands?" said Bill Ammon.

"They are there yet," said George.

"Did you think they were sunk in the sea?" said Tom Kennedy.

"It might not be very ridiculous if he did," said George, "for they have terrific earthquakes, and a good many of them."

"Of course I meant," Bill explained, "who owns them?"

"Spain says she does," said George, "and she has had them a long time, for she took possession of them about fifty years after they were discovered; but she came pretty near losing them forever about a century ago."

"How was that?" Bill inquired.

"A British force attacked them," said George, "and stormed Manila, the capital, and the city had its choice to pay five million dollars or be given up to the soldiers for plunder. It paid the money."

"Do you think that was right?" Felix Ostrom asked.

"I don't know enough about it to say," George answered; "but I suppose war is war, and when it has to be made at all it ought to be made so as to accomplish something."

"What was the name of Magellan's ship?" asked Tom Kennedy.

"He started with five ships," said George, "but four of them were lost. The largest was only eighty feet long. The one that went round the world and got home was the Victoria."

"Huh!" said Tom, "I might have known it—just like those Britishers, naming everything after their queen."

"Magellan was not a Britisher, he was Portuguese," said George. "And Queen Victoria was not born till about three hundred years after his famous voyage."

The boys burst into a roar of laughter and hooted at Tom.

"It's all very well for you to laugh," said Tom when the merriment had subsided a little, "but I'd like to know how many of you would have known that I made a blunder if George Dewey hadn't explained it to you—probably not one. I can't see that anybody but George has a right to laugh at me, and I noticed that he laughed least of all."

The boys appeared to feel the sting of Tom's argument, but at the same time they felt that any opportunity to laugh at him should be improved, because he was critical and sarcastic above all the rest. They wanted to resent his remark, but did not know of any way to do it effectively, and were all getting into ill humor when Felix Ostrom thought of a way to turn the subject and restore good feeling.

"Look here, boys," said he, "as we are talking

about the sea, and some of us intend to be sailors when we are old enough. I'd like to propose that Sandy Miller sing us a sea song. He knows a ripping good one, and I know he can sing it, for I heard him once at his house."

There was an immediate demand for the song, which was so loud and emphatic and unanimous that Sandy could not refuse.

"It's one that my great aunt, Miss Corbett, wrote," said he. "I can't remember it all, but I'll sing you a bit of it as well as I can. Ye'll just remember that I'm no Jenny Lind nor the choir of the Presbyterian church." Then he sang:

> "I've seen the waves as blue as air,
>   I've seen them green as grass;
> But I never feared their heaving yet,
>   From Grangemouth to the Bass.
> I've seen the sea as black as pitch,
>   I've seen it white as snow;
> But I never feared its foaming yet,
>   Though the waves blew high or low.
>   When sails hang flapping on the masts,
>   While through the waves we snore,
>   When in a calm we're tempest-tossed,
>   We'll go to sea no more—
>   No more—
>   We'll go to sea no more.
>
> "The sun is up, and round Inchkeith
>   The breezes softly blaw;
>   The gudeman has the lines on board—
>   Awa'! my bairns, awa'!

>   An' ye'll be back by gloamin' gray,
>   An' bright the fire will low,
>   An' in your tales and sangs we'll tell
>   How weel the boat ye row.
>   When life's last sun gaes feebly down,
>   An' death comes to our door,
>   When a' the world's a dream to us,
>   We'll go to sea no more —
>   No more —
>   We'll go to sea no more."

When the applause that greeted the song had subsided, little Steve Leonard asked: "I suppose that means they'll sail all their lives, doesn't it?"

"Yes, it means just about that," said Tom Kennedy.

Paying no attention to the touch of sarcasm in Tom's intonation, Steve added:

"Well, they might do that in a fishing boat, but they couldn't do it in the navy. My Uncle Walter is an officer in the navy, and he's got to get out of it next year, because he'll be sixty-two years old, though there isn't a gray hair in his head."

"The people in the song *were* fishermen," said Sandy.

At this moment there was a cry of alarm among the small boys in the stream. One of them had got beyond his depth and had disappeared beneath the surface.

The larger boys rushed down the bank with eager inquiries: "Where?" "Where did he go down?"

But two of them—George Dewey and Bill Ammon—did not need to wait for the answer. They knew the exact depth of every square yard in that part of the river, and the set of the current at every point, for they had been in it and through it more than a hundred times.

"Run down the bank and go in by the pine tree, Bill," said George. "I'll go in just below the riffle and explore the cellar-hole!"

A few seconds later both of these boys had disappeared under water.

The "cellar-hole," as the boys called it, was a place where some natural force, probably frost and the current, had excavated the bed of the river to a depth of eight or ten feet, with almost perpendicular walls. It was a favorite place for the larger boys to dive; and another of their amusements consisted in floating down into it with the current, which, just before entering the cellar-hole, ran swiftly through a narrow channel.

The two boys were under water so long that their companions began to fear they never would come up. From the excited state of their minds it seemed even longer than it really was.

Bill was the first to appear, and as soon as he could get his breath he reported "No luck!"

A moment later George came up, and it was evident that he was bringing something. As soon as Bill saw this he swam toward him, and at the same time two other boys plunged in from the bank. They brought ashore the apparently lifeless body of little Jimmy Nash and laid it on the grass.

"What shall we do?" said several.

"Shake the water out of him," said one.

"Stand him on his head," said another.

"Roll him over a barrel," said a third.

"Somebody run for a doctor," said a fourth; and this suggestion was quickly carried out by two of the smaller boys, who scampered off in search of a physician.

"The barrel is the right idea," said George, "but there is no barrel anywhere in sight. Boys, bring us that big log."

Half a dozen boys made a rush for the log, rolled it down the slope, and brought it to the place where it was wanted. They laid Jimmy across it, face down, and gently rolled him back and forth, which brought considerable water out of his lungs.

One of the boys who had run for a physician had the good fortune to come upon Dr. Dewey, who was passing in his gig, and shouted:

"Doctor! Doctor! there's a drownded boy down here! Come quick!"

The doctor sprang to the ground, tied his horse to the fence in less time than it takes to tell it, and followed the excited boy across the field and down the bank.

After working over the little fellow about half an hour he brought him back to consciousness, and at the end of another half hour Jimmy was well enough to be taken to his home. He was very weak, and two large boys walked beside him, supporting him by the arms, while all the others followed in a half-mournful, half-joyful procession.

"I wonder if Jimmy's father will lick him for being drowned," said Tom Kennedy.

CHAPTER III.

BATTLE ROYAL.

Winter came to Montpelier, and with it frost, snow, and a new school year.

The first snowfall was in the night, and by noon of the next day it was soft enough to pack, presenting an opportunity for fun such as American boys never forego. Big or little, studious or indolent, every one of those whose acquaintance we have made in the preceding pages, together with many of their schoolmates whom we have not named, took up handfuls of the cold, white substance, fashioned them into balls, and tried his skill at throwing. It is the Yankee form of carnival, and woe to him who fails to take the pelting good-naturedly.

That day the fun was thickest at the orchard near the schoolhouse. Half a dozen boys, partly sheltered by the low stone wall, were considered to be in a fort which a dozen others were attacking. At first it was every man for himself, "load and fire at will," but as the contest grew hotter (if that term will do for a snow battle) it was necessary to organize the work a little. So the smaller boys were directed to give their attention entirely to the making of balls, which the larger ones threw with more accuracy and force. One boy, having a notion to vary the game with an experiment, rolled up a ball twice as large as his head, managed to creep up to the wall with it, and then threw it up into the air so that it came down inside the fort. When it came down it landed on the head and shoulders of Teddy Hawkins, broke into a beautiful shower, and for a moment almost buried him out of sight. This feat of military skill received its appropriate applause, but the author of it had to pay the cost. Before he could get back to his own lines he was a target for every marksman in the fort, and at least half a dozen balls hit him, at all of which he laughed—with the exception of the one that broke on his neck and dropped its fragments inside his collar.

When there was a lull in the contest a boy looked over the wall and hailed the besiegers with:

"Boys, see who's coming up the road!"

A tall man who carried a book under his arm and apparently was in deep thought was approaching. This was Pangborn, the schoolmaster, fresh from college, still a hard student, and assumed by the boys to be their natural enemy from the simple fact that he had come there to be their teacher.

When he appeared at this interesting moment there was no need of any formal proclamation of truce between the contending forces. The instinct of the country schoolboy suggested the same thought probably to every one, whether besieger or besieged. The word passed along, "Make a lot of them, quick! and make them hard."

The little fellows whose hands were red and stinging with cold worked with double energy, and the larger ones ceased throwing at one another, stepped back to places where they were not so likely to be seen from the road, and by common consent formed an ambush for the unsuspecting teacher.

When he came within range a ball thrown by George Dewey, which knocked off his cap, was the signal for a general attack, and the next minute he thought himself in the center of a hailstorm, the hailstones being as large as country newspapers ever represent them. After the first sensation of bewilderment, he realized the situation, and being a man of quick wit, with some experience of boys, he saw what was the one proper thing to do.

Coolly laying down his book on his cap where it rested on the snow, and paying little attention to the balls that were still whizzing round him, he proceeded to make five or six, as round and solid as could be desired. Then, looking for the leader of the attack, and recognizing him in Dewey, he charged upon that youngster and delivered every ball with unerring aim. It was so good an exhibition of marksmanship that all the other combatants stood still and looked on, their appreciation of all good throwing balancing their repugnance to all teachers.

When he had delivered his last ball, which Master Dewey received courageously and good-naturedly in the breast, Mr. Pangborn picked up his book and his hat and resumed his walk, the small boys now coming to the front and sending their feeble shots after him.

"I'm afraid he's game," said Tom Kennedy.

"I'm not afraid of it, I'm glad of it," said Sim Nelson. "I want him to be game. Of course we must try to lick him, before the term's over, but I hope we won't succeed. I want the school to go on, and want to learn something. This may be my last winter, for I've got to go to a trade pretty soon. I was just getting a good start last winter. I was nearly through fractions when we licked old Higgins and he gave up the school."

"Then why do we lick the teacher at all?" said Sammy Atkinson.

"I suppose it wouldn't answer not to," said Sim. "What would the boys over in the Myers district say if we didn't give him a tug?"

"The boys in the Myers district tried it with their teacher last week, and got licked unmercifully," said Bill Ammon.

"At any rate," said Sim, "it appears to be an old and settled fashion. Father had a visit last night from a schoolmate, and they were talking over old times, and I heard them give a lively description of a fight with a teacher. After they had driven out three men in three winters, the trustees engaged a woman teacher. She was tall and strong, and not afraid of anything. Of course they couldn't fight her, because she was a woman; but all the same she laced those boys with a rawhide whenever they broke the rules. But father said she hadn't much education; she never took them beyond simple fractions, because she didn't understand arithmetic beyond that point herself. When they got there she would say, 'I think now we ought to take some review lessons; I believe in thoroughness.' And in the reading class she taught them to say So'-crates and Her'-cules, instead of Soc'-ra-tes and Her'-cu-les. Father said the boys learned lots of obedience that winter, but nothing else."

"Well, of course," said Teddy Hawkins—and his words were slow, because he was trying at the same time to bite off the end of a big stick of Spanish licorice—"if it was the custom of our forefathers— we must keep it up. But we want a good boy—to lead the fight and manage it. If we do it—in a helter-skelter way—we'll—get—licked."

"Certainly!" said Sim. "And that may be the result of it any way. Dewey's the fellow to lead the crowd and take charge of it. What do you say—will you do it, George?"

"If he does anything that we ought to lick him for, I will," said George. "But if you're going to be the ones to pick the quarrel, you may count me out."

The next day the teacher brought a mysterious parcel and laid it in his desk without undoing it. He had had charge of the school only a week, and by overlooking many occurrences that might have been taken as a deliberate challenge, he had hoped to make the boys see for themselves that he bore them no ill-will. His forbearance had been taken for timidity, and many of his pupils saw in the tall young graduate only another victim who was destined very soon to follow the vanquished teacher of the preceding winter.

Contrary to their expectations, Mr. Pangborn opened the school as usual, and made no allusion to the snowballing affair.

The first class was ordered to take position before his desk. As they filed past, one of the boys, extending his foot, tripped another. The boy that was tripped made a great fuss about it, fell unnecessarily over a bench, and professed to be hurt both in mind and in body.

Mr. Pangborn called the aggressor before him and said:

"I was willing to pass over what occurred yesterday at the orchard, and I had no intention of informing your parents about it. I recognize the fact that you are boys, and I know that boys like fun and must have it. If you sometimes misplace your fun and overdo it, and act like highwaymen instead of good, healthy, civilized boys, if it is outside the schoolhouse and school hours I have no more to say about it than any other citizen. But when you're here you've got to behave yourselves. I will say no more about what has just occurred, but at the least sign of any further riot or misbehavior I'll put a stop to it in a way that you'll remember, and this will help me."

With that he opened the parcel and displayed a large new rawhide.

For a few seconds there was a dead silence in the room. Then a boy in one of the back seats—it was George Dewey—stood up and said:

"Mr. Pangborn, I want to tell you what I think about that, and I guess most of the boys think as I do. If they don't, I hope you'll let them say what they do think. You've been giving us sums in proportion, and my father tells me I must try to apply everything I learn. If I do anything wrong I'm willing to be licked according; but I don't want to take a big thrashing for a little thing. I don't believe any boy in this school will do anything bad enough to deserve that rawhide; you can't give any but the biggest thrashings with it. And so if you attempt to use it at all we'll all turn in and lick you."

"You've made quite a good show of argument, George," said the teacher, "and I like to have a boy exercise his reasoning powers—that's one thing I'm here to teach you. But there is a serious fault or two in your statement of the case. In the first place, no boy is obliged to do any wrong, little or great; he is at perfect liberty to obey all the rules and behave like a gentleman, and if he does so he'll not be touched by this rawhide or anything else. If he chooses to break the rules he knows beforehand what it will cost him, and he has no right to complain. In the second place, the trustees have not put you here to govern the school or judge how it ought to be governed. They have employed me for that; and I intend to do what I have agreed to do and am paid' for doing. I have come here to teach the school, but I can't teach without order and obedience on the part of the pupils; and order and obedience I will have— pleasantly if I can, forcibly if I must. If you had

A schoolroom episode.

stopped, George, at the end of your argument, I should stop here with my answer, and should praise you for having reasoned out the case as well as you could, though you did not arrive at the right conclusion. Nothing will please me better than for the boys to cultivate a habit of doing their own thinking and learn to think correctly. You will always find me ready to listen to reason. But you did not stop at the end of your argument; you added a threat to attack me with the whole school to help you and overcome me. Whatever you may say of big and little faults, you have now committed one of the greatest. If I passed over such a breach of discipline, my usefulness here would be at an end. Unless I am master there can be no school. If you see the justice of this and are manly enough to acknowledge it, you may simply stand up and apologize for your threat, and then we'll go on with the lessons as if nothing had happened. If not, of course you must take the consequences."

"I don't know how to apologize," said George, "and I'm not going to."

"Then step out here," said the teacher, as he took up the rawhide.

The boy went forward at once, with his fists clenched and his eyes blazing.

Mr. Pangborn saw there was good stuff in him,

if only it were properly cultivated, and could not repress a feeling of admiration for his courage.

"Now let's see you strike me," said George.

The next instant the rawhide came down across his shoulders, and with a cry of rage the boy threw himself upon his teacher, fighting like a terrier.

Then five or six of the larger boys came to George's aid; most of the smaller ones followed them; those who were not anxious to fight did their part by yelling, overthrowing desks, and spilling ink; and the whole place was in a hideous uproar. They charged upon the teacher from all sides, but he held fast to Dewey's collar with one hand while he plied the rawhide with the other. The largest boy, who had received a stinging cut across the face, got a stick from the wood-box and let it fly at the master's head, which it narrowly missed. Feeling that his life might be in danger, Mr. Pangborn picked up the stick and waded into the crowd, using it as a policeman uses his club. The boy who had thrown it was toppled over with a blow on the head, and in three minutes all the others were driven out of the schoolhouse, some of them feeling a little lame about the shoulders and sides—all except Dewey, on whom the teacher had not relaxed his grip. He now resumed the rawhide and gave the boy as much more as he thought he deserved.

A little later they left the house together and walked up the street to Dr. Dewey's office, where the boy was turned over to his father, with a brief statement of the circumstances. Dr. Dewey thanked the teacher for what he had done, and the lesson to George was complete.

The next morning George was in his seat at the tap of the bell, and throughout the day he was as orderly and studious as could be desired. When the session was over and the teacher was leaving the house, he found the boy waiting for him at the door. George extended his hand and said:

"Father and I talked that matter all over, and we both came to the conclusion that you did exactly right. I thank you for it."

From that time Zenas K. Pangborn and George Dewey were fast friends.

CHAPTER IV.

EDUCATION AT NORWICH.

A year later George Dewey left the school and went to the Morrisville Academy, and there also Mr. Pangborn's teachings stood him in good stead. His aptitude in sports always made Dewey a favorite with his companions. He was one of the fastest runners and the best skaters, and he had the knack of doing everything he did quickly and neatly, in the way that shows the properly balanced relations between mind and eye and body. He acted as he thought— quickly and surely—and he was certain to resent any insult or infringement of what he considered his rights.

Dr. Dewey had been thinking over his son's future, and had decided upon sending George to West Point, although even at this time the boy's inclinations turned more strongly to the other branch of the service. Yet he did not strenuously object, and so after a year at Morrisville he was sent to Norwich University at Northfield, Vermont.

Norwich University stands on a plateau above the town of Northfield. It is a fine old place, with a wide parade-ground extending before the buildings, and back of it are the brick barracks that contain the cadets' quarters and the armory and recitation rooms. Everything was managed in military fashion, and there was no better school in which to fit a boy for the life and habits of a soldier. It was in the year 1851 that George Dewey became a pupil there, and from the day of his coming he manifested the powers of leadership that afterward distinguished him.

Four or five young fellows in uniform were seated in one of the rooms in the South Barrack. They belonged to the second-year men, and the second year at any institution of learning is perhaps the crucial one. If a boy gets into any mischief that is serious, it is generally in his second year. The doings of the sophomore have cost many a dollar out of the college treasury, to pay for stolen gates and burned fences, smashed lamp-posts and injured constables. And it was so with the second year's men at Norwich.

"Where's Doc. Dewey?" asked one of the boys. "We must get him into the scheme, or the whole thing will fall through."

"If any of you fellows want to see Doc. Dewey, all you've got to do is to come to the window," said a boy who was gazing out on the parade ground.

At the farther end a solitary figure was patrolling up and down, turning at the end of his beat about a large elm that stood in the corner of the campus. The punishments at Norwich were of a military character, and extra sentry duty was the reward for any breach of discipline.

"I ought to be the one doing all that marching," said one of the boys, "for George only tried to get me out of the scrape, but he wouldn't let me tell."

"Well, he'll be off in half an hour," said another, "and we'll meet in his rooms. What do you say?"

"So say we all of us," was the return. "We can hatch up the scheme there better than anywhere else."

In a few minutes the party broke up, to meet later in a room down the hallway.

Across the Connecticut River, which skirts the town of Northfield, is the town of Hanover, the seat of old Dartmouth College. From time immemorial the greatest rivalry had existed between the two institutions, and in the years that preceded the civil war this feeling had almost grown into a feud, and for a member of either institution to cross the river was to enter the enemy's country, with all the attendant risk. Only three or four evenings previously Dewey and one of the other cadets had boldly crossed the bridge and appeared in the Hanover streets in broad daylight. It had not taken long for the news to reach the ears of a few of the Dartmouth sophomores, who were spoiling for a row, and soon Dewey and his

companions had found out that they were followed.
But it was not until they had reached the entrance
to the bridge that there was any sign of trouble.
There, sure enough, they saw four of the Dartmouth
belligerents waiting for them. An old farmer, crossing
the bridge from Hanover to Northfield, was driving
a pair of rather skittish horses that were prancing as
they heard the rattling of the boards beneath their
feet. It was almost time for the evening assembly,
and if the boys were to be prompt they must not be
stopped, although such, it was plain, was the intention
of the Dartmouth boys who were awaiting them.
They asked the farmer if he would give them a ride,
and he declined; but they had jumped into the wagon,
and, when near the spot where their four enemies had
lined across the causeway, one of the cadets leaned
forward and, picking up the whip, struck the two
horses across their backs. This was all they needed;
the Dartmouth boys had barely time to jump aside
when the team went tearing by. But it was easier
to get the young horses going than to stop them.
The rattling of the bridge frightened them more and
more, and the people on the streets of Northfield were
surprised to see a runaway come roaring into town
with an old man and two hatless cadets hauling at
the reins without result. It was fortunate that no
harm was done, and the horses were stopped halfway

up the hill that leads to the University; but the president had seen and recognized the two uniformed figures, and that was one reason why Doc. Dewey was walking about the old elm on this fine spring day.

The evening before, one of the cadets had returned from a nocturnal excursion across the river with his coat torn and a story of being badly treated. Revenge was being planned, and the plotters had chosen Dewey as their leader for the coming expedition that was meant to teach the Dartmouth fellows a lesson. This expedition resulted in a lively encounter, in which, though outnumbered, the Norwich boys are said to have been victorious. In the traditions of the school it is known as the Battle of the Torn Coats.

In Dewey's last year at Norwich the faculty procured two fine six-pounder howitzers, with limbers, to replace the old iron guns at which the cadets had been exercised. When they arrived, the cadets took down the old guns and brought up the new ones from the railway station. As boys naturally would, they divided into two parties and made a frolic of the occasion. It was tedious work getting the guns out of the car, but as soon as they were out and limbered up the fun began. One of the cadets has told the story very prettily in his diary.

"Ainsworth and Munson chose squads to draw them to the parade. I chanced to be in Ainsworth's squad. Ainsworth's squad wanted to lead, but as Munson's squad had the road ahead and we were at the side and in sandy gutters, it was doubtful how we were to do it. They started off with a fine spurt, getting a big lead. Going up the hill where the road was broader we steadily gained until only the length of the trail in the rear; then we gathered and started on a run, passing and keeping the lead, with cheers and great glee. Climbing the hill, we proceeded more slowly, Munson quietly in the rear, on our way round the North Barracks and then through the usual gateway to position. As we entered the village near the southeast corner of the parade, we noticed Munson's squad, apparently under the lead of Dewey, making for a short cut across the grounds, first breaking down the fence for passage. Now our efforts were redoubled, and the boys of the other squad declare that they never saw fellows run as we ran, or expect to see a gun jump as that six-pounder bounded along the main street and around the corner. But we led; round the North Barracks at double quick went gun and gun squad, entered the barrack yard and placed the gun in position before the west front of the South Barracks, giving three cheers for No. 1 to the chagrin of No. 2, just approaching position.

It was a great race and pleased the faculty exceedingly."

This was only one of many episodes that prevented life at Norwich from being dull for the boys, and sweetened their memories in after time, though not assisting directly in any useful branch of education.

CHAPTER V.

LIFE AT ANNAPOLIS.

WHEN Dr. Dewey had consented to his son's wishes for a naval education, the next step was to secure his appointment to a cadetship at the Academy at Annapolis. Each member of Congress has the privilege of appointing a candidate when there is no cadet from his district in the Academy; and the President has ten appointments at large, besides one for the District of Columbia. The giving of these appointments after a competitive examination was not so common forty years ago as it is now. They were almost invariably bestowed arbitrarily, according to the Congressman's personal relations with those who sought them or his idea of his own political interests. But it was of little use to appoint a boy who could not pass the mental and physical entrance examinations. George Dewey obtained an appointment, but only as alternate. The first place was given to a schoolmate two years older than he, George B. Spalding. For some reason Spalding, though a bright boy, failed to pass, while the alternate answered the requirements and was admitted to the Academy. Mr. Spalding was graduated two years later at the University of Vermont, studied theology at Andover, and has had a creditable career as a clergyman and legislator. It is said that only about forty per cent of the appointees are able to pass the entrance examinations, and of those who are admitted, only about half finish the course.

Dewey entered the Academy September 23, 1854, being then in his seventeenth year. He was born December 26, 1837. The number of cadets was then one hundred and sixty, the curriculum had been recently remodeled for a four-years' course, and the first class under the new regulation was graduated that year. Captain Louis M. Goldsborough (afterward rear admiral) was the superintendent.

The classes are designated by numbers, the lowest (corresponding to freshmen in a college) being called the fourth. The cadets (or midshipmen, as they were then called; that term is no longer in use) were under the immediate charge of an officer called the Commandant of Midshipmen. He ranked next to the superintendent, and was the executive officer of the institution and the instructor in seamanship, gunnery, and naval tactics. He had three assistants. There were eight professorships—Mathematics; Astronomy, Navigation and Surveying; Natural and Experimental

Philosophy; Field Artillery and Infantry Tactics; Ethics and English Studies; French; Spanish; and Drawing.

The examinations of all the classes were held in February and June. A very strict record was kept of the conduct of every student; and after the June examination those in the second class who had not received more than a hundred and fifty demerit marks during the year were furloughed till October, while the others were at once embarked for the annual practice cruise. This appears like a great number of demerit marks for even the worst student to receive, but some offenses were punished with more than one mark. Thus, for neglect of orders or overstaying leave of absence the penalty was ten marks; for having a light in one's room after taps, eight; for absence from parade or roll call, six; for slovenly dress, four, etc. Any cadet who received more than two hundred demerits in a year was dropped from the rolls; and it was optional with the superintendent to dismiss a cadet from the service for being intoxicated or having liquor in his possession; for going beyond the limits of the institution without permission; for giving, carrying, or accepting a challenge; for playing at cards or any game of chance in the Academy; for offering violence or insult to a person on public duty; for publishing anything relating to the Academy; or for any conduct unbecoming a gentleman.

The daily routine of the Academy is of interest as showing to what discipline the cadets were subjected, and what habits of promptness, regularity, and accuracy were cultivated. Marshall's History of the Academy shows us what it was at that time, and it is still practically the same.

The morning gun-fire and reveille with the beating of the drum was at 6.15 A. M., or at 6.30, according to the season. Then came the police of quarters and inspection of rooms. The roll call was at 6.45 or at 7.15, according to the season. From December 1st to March 1st the later hour was the one observed. Chapel service followed, and afterward breakfast at 7 or at 7.30. The sick call was thirty minutes after breakfast. Then the cadets had recreation till 8 o'clock, when the study and recitation hours began.

Section formations took place in the front hall of the third floor, under the supervision of the officer of the day, who, as well as the section leaders, was responsible for preservation of silence and order. When the signal was given by the bugle, the sections were marched to their recitation rooms. They marched in close order, in silence, and with strict observance of military decorum. Whenever a section left its recitation room it was marched by its leader to the third floor, and there dismissed.

Study alternated or intervened with recitations

until one o'clock, when the signal for dinner was given. The cadets were again formed in order by the captains of crews, and marched into the mess hall. The organization was into ten guns' crews, for instruction in seamanship and gunnery, and for discipline. The captains of crews, when at the mess table, repressed promptly all disorderly conduct, unbecoming language, and unnecessary noise. They enforced perfect silence among their guns' crews until the order " Seats! " had been given. Then conversation was permitted. Silence was enforced again after the order " Rise! " until the crews reached the main hall. At all times, in mustering their crews, the captains were required to call the names in the lowest tone that would secure attention. They were required to report any irregularity in uniform or untidiness which they perceived at any formation, as well as any infraction of regulations, disregard of orders, or other impropriety.

The Professor of Field Artillery and Infantry Tactics was inspector of the mess hall, and presided at the mess table. He had charge of the police and order of the mess hall, in which duty he was assisted by the officer of the day and the captains of crews. Each student had a seat assigned to him at table, which he could not change without the sanction of the inspector of the mess hall; and no student must appear at meals negligently dressed.

Thirty minutes were allowed for breakfast, and the same time for supper. Forty minutes were allowed for dinner.

After dinner the young gentlemen had recreation again until two o'clock, when the afternoon study and recitation hours began. These continued until four o'clock, followed by instruction in the art of defense, infantry or artillery drill, and recreation until parade and roll call at sunset. Supper followed immediately; then recreation and call to evening studies at 6.25 or 6.55, according to the season. Study hours continued until tattoo at half past nine, which was a signal for extinguishing lights and inspection of rooms. After "taps" at ten o'clock no lights were allowed in any part of the students' quarters, except by authority of the superintendent.

On the school-ship attached to the Academy there was another set of rules and regulations, concerning duty, conduct, and etiquette, so minute and exacting that one would think it was a liberal education merely to learn them all, to say nothing of obeying them daily and hourly. Here are the greater part of them:

At reveille the midshipmen will immediately turn out, arrange their bedding, and taking the lashing from the head clews of their hammocks, where it was neatly coiled the night before, will lash up their hammocks, taking seven taut turns at equal distances, and tucking in their clews neatly. They will then place their hammocks under their right arms, and first captains will give the order, "Stand by your hammocks, No. — forward, march!" at which order they will proceed in line, by their allotted ladders, to their allotted places in their respective nettings; when there, they will in order deliver their hammocks to those appointed to receive them. Each first captain delivering his hammock and falling back, will face the line of his gun's crew, and see that proper order is maintained; each midshipman, after delivering his hammock, will fall back, facing outboard, forming line from first captain aft. When all are stowed, the first captains, each at the head of his crew, will face them in the direction of their ladder, and march them to the wash room—odd-numbered crews on starboard, even numbers on port side of the wash room. Towels will be marked and kept in their places, over each respective basin. No one will leave the wash room until marched out; three guns' crews will wash at the same time, and each week the numbers will be changed. When ready, the first captains will march their crews to their places on the berth deck, where they will dismiss them.

Guns' crews Nos. 1 and 2 stow hammocks in forward netting—No. 2 on port, and No. 1 on starboard side; Nos. 3, 5, and 7 in starboard, and Nos. 4, 6, and 8 in port quarter-deck nettings, lowest numbers of each crew stowing forward.

Nos. 1 and 2 guns' crews leave berth deck by fore-hatch ladders, Nos. 3 and 4 by main-hatch ladders, Nos. 5 and 6 by after-hatch ladders, and Nos. 7 and 8 by steerage ladders, each on their respective sides, and each march to their allotted places on spar deck.

Twelve minutes from the close of reveille (which will be shown by three taps on the drum) are allowed for lashing hammocks and to leave the berth deck.

The guns' crews will form in two ranks, at their respective places on gun deck: Nos. 1, 3, 5, and 7 on port side, and Nos. 2, 4, 6, and 8 on starboard side; first and second captains on the right of their crews, officer in charge, and adjutant forward of main-mast. Officer of the day and superintendents forward of main hatch, fronting officer in charge; when formed they will be faced to the front, and dressed by first captains by the orders, "Front; right dress." The adjutant then gives the order, "Muster your crews!" when each first captain, taking one step to the front, faces the line of his crew, second captain stepping forward into his interval; first captain then calls the roll from memory, noting absentees; when finished, faces toward his place, second captain takes backward step to his former position, and first captain faces about to his place in the front rank; the adjutant then gives the order, "First captains front and center!" First captains take one full step to the front, and face the adjutant's position, second captains filling intervals as before; the adjutant then gives the order, "March!" at which captains march in direction of the adjutant, forming in line abreast of him. The adjutant then gives the order, "Front! report!" The captains report all present, thus: "All present, No. 1!" or, if any are absent, thus: "——absent, No. 1!" First captain of No. 1 will begin in a short, sharp, and intelligible tone, making the salute when he has finished, which will be the signal for first captain of No. 2 to report, and so on to the last. The adjutant then gives the order, "Posts! march!" the first captains facing, at the order "posts!" in the direction of their crews, advance at the word "march!" to their places in the ranks. The adjutant then reports to the officer in charge, and receives his instructions; if there be any orders he publishes them; he then gives the order, "Two files from the right, two paces to the front, march!" when the two files from the right of each rank step two paces to the front, and the adjutant gives the order, "Battalion right dress!" The battalion dresses on the two files, and the adjutant gives the order, "Battalion to the rear, open order, march!" when the rear rank will take two steps to the rear, halt, and be dressed by the second captain.

The officer in charge, with the adjutant, will proceed to inspect the battalion. The adjutant will then give the order, "Rear rank, close order, march!" when the rear rank will take two steps forward. The adjutant then gives the order, "Officer of the day and superintendents, relieve!" at which the officer of the day and superintendents of the day previous will face about, and pass the orders to their reliefs, the officer of the day delivering his side arms; they will then take position in their respective crews.

When the officer of the day and superintendents of the day previous have taken their places in their crews, the adjutant gives the order, "March to breakfast!" the first captains will direct their crews by their respective ladders to their respective mess tables. On arriving at the mess tables, each first captain will take position in rear of his camp stool, at the after end of the table, second captain taking the forward end, and the crew taking position corresponding to their places in the ranks; all will remain standing in rear of their respective camp stools until the officer in charge gives the order, "Seats!" at which word the midshipmen will place their caps under their camp stools, and quietly take their seats. As the midshipmen at each table shall have finished the meal, the first captain will rise and look at the adjutant, who will acknowledge the report by raising his right hand;

the first captain will then resume his seat; when all shall have reported, the adjutant will make it known to the officer in charge, who, rising from his seat, will tap on the table and give the order, " Rise!" at which order each midshipman will rise, put on his cap, step to the rear of his camp stool, putting it in place, and facing aft; at the order " March!" from the adjutant, first captains will advance, followed by their crews in their proper order, and proceed to their parade stations on the gun deck, where they will form and dress their command, and bring them to parade rest in order for prayers. All will take off their caps at the opening of prayers, and put them on at the order " Attention!" at the close of prayers, from the adjutant, who gives the order " Battalion, attention! right face, break ranks, march!"

The hours for recitation and study were the same on board the training ship as in quarters—from about eight o'clock in the morning to one o'clock, and from about two o'clock in the afternoon to four o'clock. The guns' crews were then assembled for exercise at the great guns for an hour or more, or perhaps in infantry drill, or in practical seamanship, including exercises with boats, the lead, log, etc. Evening parade intervened, and after supper the fourth class were called to their studies again. At tattoo, half past nine in the evening, the midshipmen were required to arrange their books and papers neatly, place their chairs under their desks, and at gun-fire form by crews, when the officer in charge inspected the study tables. At "taps" all must turn in, and all noise must cease at four bells.

The rules of etiquette were very minute. Here are some of them:

The midshipmen will not use the steerage ladders, the after ladder from the gun deck, the starboard poop ladder, the starboard side of the poop, quarter-deck, or gangway abaft No. 2 recitation room; they are particularly enjoined to keep the starboard gangway clear. The etiquette of the quarter-deck will be strictly observed. Officers on coming up the quarter-deck ladders will make the salute. No running, skylarking, boisterous conduct, or loud talking will be permitted on the quarter-deck or poop. The midshipmen will never appear on the gun deck or quarter-deck without their caps, jackets, and cravats. They will, in ascending and descending the ladders, avoid the heavy step upon them which is made by shore people; when absent in boats they will yield implicit and prompt obedience to their captains, or those placed in charge. It is particularly forbidden to get out of or into the ship through the ports, or to sit on the rail of the ship. No one is permitted to go out on the head-booms during study hours, or to go aloft, without authorized permission. No one is permitted to go or come from the berth deck during study hours by any other than the main-hatch ladders. The midshipmen are forbidden to sit upon the study tables.

A young man who could go through with four years of such discipline as this, and at the same time keep up such proficiency in his studies as to pass the examinations, might well be supposed to be thoroughly fitted for the duties of life. George Dewey went through with it, and on graduation, in 1858, stood fifth in a class of fourteen. His classmate, Captain Henry L. Howison, says of him: " In his studies Dewey was exceedingly bright. At graduation he was No. 5 in our class and I was No. 4, but after the rearrangement at the end of our final cruise he was No. 4 and I was No. 5. He was a born fighter. He was just as much of a fighter in a small way when he was a boy as he has been in a large way as a man. His days at the Naval Academy proved this. He is quick at the trigger and has a strong temper, but he has excellent control over it. When a cadet he would always fight, and fight hard if necessary, but he was never known to be in a brawl. I do not want to convey the idea that he ever wanted to get into a row, because he didn't. He would go a long way to get out of fighting if the affair was none of his business. He was sure to be on the right side of every fight, but the fight had to come to him. He did not seek it. If he saw a quarrel on the street and he thought it the part of a gentleman to help one or the other of the contestants, he would not hesitate a moment about pitching in. He would go miles to help a friend who was in trouble. He was fond of animals, and especially fond of horses. Ever since I have known him he has gone horseback riding whenever he had a chance, and has owned several fine animals. At the Academy he would ride whenever he could get anything to ride. He had a fine horse when we lived in Washington. I recall that Dewey as a lad was very fond of music, and, indeed, quite a musician himself. He had a really good baritone voice, nearly a tenor, and he used it well and frequently, too. He also played the guitar well. He was no soloist, but could play accompaniments all right."

When Dewey was in the Academy there was a special source of misunderstanding, ill feeling, and quarrels in the heated condition of politics and sectional jealousy; and then, as ever, it was customary for the boys to settle their differences with their natural means of offense and defense. Dewey did not escape the peculiar peril of those days. There is a story to the effect that the leader of the Southern party among the cadets made an occasion to give George an unmistakable statement of his opinion of Yankees in general and George in particular, whereupon he presently found himself provided with a black eye. Then came a challenge to mortal combat, which George promptly accepted. Seconds were chosen, and a meeting would undoubtedly have taken place had not some of the students informed the faculty, who put a stop to the scheme and made the boys give their word of honor to keep the peace.

George participated in the annual practice cruises with his classmates, and after graduation they were sent on a two-years' cruise in European waters in the steam frigate Wabash, commanded by Captain Samuel Barron. The ship attracted a great deal of attention in every port she visited. Steam had been only recently adopted for naval vessels, and the Americans had constructed a type of steam frigate that was superior to anything in the other navies of the world. While the Wabash lay at Malta a fine steam yacht came in from the sea and anchored near her. It was said that she was the property of a distinguished nobleman, and was one of the few first-class steam yachts then in existence. She excited a great deal of curiosity among the officers of the Wabash. A few days later Captain Barron gave out a general invitation, and many visitors from the garrison and from British men-of-war in the harbor came to inspect the new war ship from the West. Dewey and the other midshipmen were on hand to assist in doing the honors, and when a kindly-looking gentleman with a small party came up the gangway and saluted the quarter-deck with a nautical air, George returned the salute and asked if he could be of any service. The gentleman said he would like to see whatever was to be seen, and the self-possessed young midshipman proceeded to show him and his party over the vessel. When they had nearly completed the rounds, Dewey ventured to offer his card by way of introduction. The gentleman took out his own card and gave it in return, and Dewey, as he glanced at it, read one of the highest names in the British peerage. "Yes," said the gentleman, "that is my little teakettle anchored under your quarter. I fear she'll seem rather cramped after we go aboard of her from this." Dewey's conscience now began to trouble him, and he insisted on taking the party to his commanding officer, though, as he anticipated, from that moment his own existence was ignored.

While nothing strictly historical took place in connection with this cruise, there were many pleasant incidents and some that made strong impressions on the young midshipmen in regard to duty and discipline. Several Italian ports were visited, princes and ambassadors were received on board, and courtesies were exchanged with the war vessels of several nations. The Fourth of July and Washington's Birthday were duly observed, and on the former occasion one of the officers read the Declaration of Independence to the ship's company assembled on deck. At Leghorn the Wabash ran aground, and a British merchant steamer assisted in getting her off. At Genoa some of the petty officers and seamen got into a street fight, in which a man was killed; and the captain sent them all ashore next day for the civil authorities to identify the participants. At Spezia, Dewey records in his journal, " five hundred and fifty gallons of beans were surveyed, condemned, and thrown overboard," furnished probably by contract. This is in striking contrast with what afterward he was able to say concerning the supplies of the fleet at Manila. On November 13, 1859, they sailed for home, and on December 16th arrived at the port of New York. A little later Midshipman Dewey was examined at Annapolis for a commission, and he not only passed the examination, but was advanced in his relative standing. He then received leave of absence to visit his home. He was commissioned lieutenant April 19, 1861, and was ordered to the steam sloop Mississippi.

CHAPTER VI.

THE BEGINNING OF WAR.

THE United States navy had done little to distinguish itself since its wonderful achievements in the War of 1812 with Great Britain. During the Mexican War it took part in the occupation of California, and performed what service it could in the Gulf, but there was no opportunity for anything remarkable. Wilkes had made his exploring expedition in Pacific and Antarctic waters; Ingraham, in the St. Louis, had demanded and secured the release of Martin Koszta at Smyrna; Tatnall, with his famous "blood is thicker than water," had participated in the bombardment of the Chinese forts at Peiho; Hudson, in the Niagara, had assisted in laying the first Atlantic cable; and several cruisers had pursued pirates in the West Indies. But with the exception of these occurrences the navy had done nothing to attract popular attention for more than forty years. Yet it had quietly accomplished much good work on the Coast Survey; and the Naval Academy at Annapolis, from its establishment in 1845, educated officers who gave character and efficiency to the service, and when the day of battle came showed themselves to be worthy successors of the famous captains who had preceded them.

A great crisis in the nation's history was now approaching, more rapidly than any one suspected. The older statesmen were gone. Adams, Jackson, Clay, Calhoun, and Webster, all had passed away within a period of seven years. Their successors were men of different mold, and the problem that had given them the most serious trouble, while comparatively small in their day, had now grown to monstrous proportions. The difficulty arose from the existence of two exactly opposite systems of labor in the two parts of the country. In the Southern States the laborers were of a different race from the capitalists and ruling class, and were slaves; in the Northern States all (except a very small proportion) were of the white race and all were free. The different ideas and interests that arose from these two different states of society had constantly tended to alienate the people of one section from those of the other, and the frequent clashing of these interests in the halls of legislation had obscured the fact that in a much larger view, and for permanent reasons, the interests and destiny of the whole country were the same. In the summer when young Dewey was graduated at the Naval Academy, Abraham Lincoln, then in the midst of a heated canvass on this question, said in a speech that became famous: " I believe this Government can not endure permanently half slave and half free. I do not expect the Union to be dissolved, I do not expect the house to fall, but I do expect it will cease to be divided. It will become all one thing, or all the other." Most of the Southern statesmen, and a few of those at the North, looked to a division of the country as the best, if not the inevitable, solution of the problem. But against this there was a barrier greater and more permanent than any wording of constitution or laws enacted in the last century by a generation that had passed away. This was the geography of our country. Mr. Lincoln did not distinctly name it as the reason for his faith in the perpetuity of the Union, but he probably felt it. History shows unmistakably that the permanent boundaries of a country are the geographical ones. Conquest or diplomacy occasionally establishes others, but they do not endure. Separate tribes or peoples, if living within the same geographical boundaries, ultimately come together and form one nation. Had our country been crossed from east to west by a great river like the Amazon, or a chain of lakes like those that separate us from Canada, or a high mountain range, the northern and southern sections might never have come together, or would have been easily separated into two distinct peoples. But with no such natural line of division, and with the Mississippi running south through the center of the country, and with railroads, telegraphs, and other rapidly multiplying means of communication tying the sections together, the perpetuity of the Union was a foregone conclusion, whatever might be the arguments of the politician or the passions of the people.

Nevertheless, the struggle had to come, whether this great consideration was realized or not, and come it did. The Southern statesmen were in earnest in their threat of disunion, and when Abraham Lincoln was elected to the presidency in 1860 they proceeded to carry it out. South Carolina passed an ordinance of secession in December, and most of the other Southern States followed quickly, and the new government, called the Confederate States of America, was organized at Montgomery, Alabama, in February, 1861. They proceeded to take possession of the United States forts, arsenals, and navy yards within their territory, and soon had them all without firing a gun, except those at Pensacola and Fort Sumter in Charleston harbor. The Confederate forces erected several batteries within reach of Sumter, and on April 12th opened fire on the fort and compelled its surrender. This was the actual beginning of hostilities, and within twenty-four hours the whole country, North and

South, was ablaze with the war spirit. The President called for volunteers to suppress the rebellion and restore the national authority, and was offered several times as many as he asked for. The South was already in arms. Many of the military and naval officers who were from the South went with their States, and young men who had been educated together at West Point or Annapolis were now to take part on opposite sides in one of the greatest conflicts the world has ever seen. In some instances brother was against brother, and father against son.

Gideon Welles, of Connecticut, was Secretary of the Navy in President Lincoln's cabinet. Though some of the naval officers resigned their commissions and offered their services to the Confederacy, the vessels of the navy, except a very few that were captured at Norfolk navy yard, remained in the possession of the National Government. There was need of all these and more, for a mighty task was about to be undertaken, and there were large bodies of troops to be transported by sea, cities to be captured, fortifications to be bombarded, and ports to be held under blockade. This last was a most important duty, though little idea of glory was connected with it, and popular reputations could not be made in it; for the Southern States had very few manufactures, and for arms, ammunition, and other necessaries they depended mainly on importation.

At this time the United States navy was undergoing transformation. In the more important vessels steam had been substituted for sail power, but they were still constructed of wood, and the development of the ironclad was just beginning. In the emergency the Government bought a large number of merchant vessels of various kinds, including some ferryboats, turning them into gunboats and transports, and began the construction of ironclads. Many ironclads of light draught for use on the western rivers were built in a hundred days. The Southerners were almost without facilities for building vessels from the keel, but they made two or three formidable rams and floating batteries by covering the wooden hulls of some of the captured ships with railroad iron.

The first naval expedition of the war sailed in August, 1861, commanded by Flag-Officer Silas H. Stringham. It consisted of ten vessels, including two transports, carried about nine hundred soldiers, and was directed against the forts that guarded Hatteras Inlet, North Carolina. The troops, with some difficulty, were landed through the surf, and a combined attack by them and the naval force reduced the defenses and compelled their surrender with about seven hundred prisoners. The garrisons had lost about fifty men, the assailants not one. This was due to the fact that the work was done chiefly by rifled guns on the vessels, which could be fired effectively while out of range of the smooth-bore guns of the forts.

Late in October another expedition, commanded by Flag-Officer Samuel F. Du Pont, sailed from Hampton Roads. It consisted of more than fifty vessels, and carried twenty-two thousand men. A terrific gale was encountered, one transport and one storeship were lost, and one gunboat had to throw its battery overboard. When the storm was over, only one vessel was in sight from the flagship. But the scattered fleet slowly came together again and proceeded to its destination—the entrance to Port Royal harbor, South Carolina. This was guarded by two forts. The attack was made on the morning of November 7th. The main column, of ten vessels, led by the flagship, was formed in line a ship's-length apart, and steamed past the larger fort, delivering its fire at a distance of eight hundred yards, and then turned and sailed past again, somewhat closer. In this manner it steamed three times round a long ellipse, delivering its fire alternately from the two broadsides. Some of the gunboats got positions from which they enfiladed the work, and two of the larger vessels went up closer and poured in a fire that dismounted several

guns. This was more than the garrison could endure, and they evacuated the fort and were seen streaming out of it as if in panic. The other column, of four vessels, attacked the smaller fort in the same manner, with the same result.

Meanwhile, a much larger and more important naval expedition than either of these was planned at Washington. New Orleans was the largest and richest city in the Confederacy. It had nearly one hundred and seventy thousand inhabitants—more than Charleston, Mobile, and Richmond together. In the year before the war it had shipped twenty-five million dollars' worth of sugar and ninety-two million dollars' worth of cotton. In these two articles its export trade was larger than that of any other city in the world. And as a strategic point it was of the first importance. The Mississippi has several mouths, or passes, and this fact, with the frequency of violent gales in the Gulf, made it very difficult to blockade commerce there. Moreover, if possession of the Mississippi could be secured by the national forces it would cut the Confederacy in two and render it difficult if not impossible to continue the transportation of supplies from Arkansas and Texas to feed the armies in Virginia and Tennessee. Add to this the fact that any great city is a great prize in war, highly valuable to the belligerent that holds it, and the importance of New Orleans at that time may be readily appreciated.

The defenses of the city consisted of two forts—Jackson and St. Philip—on either bank of the stream, thirty miles above the head of the passes and about twice that distance below New Orleans. They were below a bend which had received the name of English Turn, from the circumstance that in 1814 the British naval vessels attempting to ascend the stream had here been driven back by land batteries. The forts were built by the United States Government, of earth and brick, in the style that was common before the introduction of rifled cannon. They were now garrisoned by fifteen hundred Confederate soldiers, and above them lay a Confederate fleet of fifteen vessels, including an ironclad ram and an incomplete floating battery that was cased in railroad iron. Below the forts a heavy chain was stretched across the river, supported on logs; and when it was broken by a freshet the logs were replaced by hulks anchored at intervals across the stream, with the chain passing over their decks and its ends fastened to trees on the banks. A similar chain was stretched across the Hudson at the time of the Revolutionary War. In addition to all this, two hundred Confederate sharpshooters constantly patrolled the banks between the forts and the head of the passes, to give notice of any approaching foe, and fire at any one that might be seen on the deck of a hostile vessel. The Confederate authorities fully appreciated the value of the Crescent City. The problem before the national authorities was, how to take that city in spite of all these barriers.

CHAPTER VII.

THE FIGHT FOR NEW ORLEANS.

MILITARY scholarship is a good thing; military genius is sometimes a better thing. When it was resolved by the authorities to attempt the capture of New Orleans it was assumed that the two forts on the river below the city must be first destroyed or compelled to surrender. The chief engineer of the Army of the Potomac, whose ability was unquestioned, made a long report to the Navy Department, in which, after describing the forts and their situation, he said: "To pass these works merely with a fleet and appear before New Orleans is merely a raid, no capture." And in describing the exact method of attack he said: "Those [vessels] on the Fort Jackson side would probably have to make fast to the shore; those on the Saint Philip side might anchor." Substantially the same view was afterward taken by Captain David D. Porter, who was to have an important part in the enterprise. It was also assumed that the forts could be reduced by bombardment, if this was only heavy and persistent enough. In accordance with this idea,

Farragut and Dewey.

twenty-one large mortars were cast for the work. They threw shells that were thirteen inches in diameter and weighed two hundred and eighty-five pounds. For each of these mortars a schooner was built; and so great was the concussion of the atmosphere when one was fired, that no man could stand near it without being literally deafened. Therefore platforms projecting beyond the decks were provided, to which the gunners could retreat just before each shot. The remainder of the fleet, when finally it was mustered, was made up of six sloops of war, sixteen gunboats, five other vessels, and transports carrying fifteen thousand soldiers to co-operate in the attack or hold the forts and the city after it should be captured. The number of guns in the fleet was more than two hundred.

After this expedition (the most powerful that ever had sailed under the American flag) was planned and partly organized, and the mortar schooners nearly completed, the Navy Department looked about for a suitable officer to command it, and Secretary Welles finally chose Captain David G. Farragut. This officer had his own ideas of the best way to effect the capture. He would have preferred to dispense with the mortars, in which he had no faith; but they had been prepared at great expense, and that part of the fleet was to be commanded by his friend Porter, and so he accepted them, and as soon as it could be got ready the expedition sailed from Hampton Roads.

When it arrived at the mouths of the Mississippi there was a gigantic task to be performed before the fleet could enter the stream. An American poet has thus described the delta of the great river:

> "Do you know of the dreary land,
>   If land such region may seem,
> Where 'tis neither sea nor strand,
> Ocean nor good dry land,
>   But the nightmare marsh of a dream—
> Where the mighty river his death-road takes,
> Mid pools and windings that coil like snakes—
> A hundred leagues of bayous and lakes—
>   To die in the great Gulf Stream?"

There are five mouths or passes, spread out like the fingers of a hand. Of course no one of them was as large and deep as the river above, and the entrance of each was obstructed by a bar. The smaller vessels —mortar schooners and gunboats—were taken in without difficulty, but the larger ones required enormous labor to get them over the bar. The Mississippi—of which Captain Melancton Smith was the commander, and Lieutenant George Dewey the executive officer—was lightened of everything that could be taken off, and even then had to be dragged over by tugboats, with her keel a foot deep in the mud. She was the only side-wheel war vessel in the fleet.

It required two weeks' labor to get the Pensacola in; and the Colorado could not be taken in at all, as she drew seven feet more of water than there was on the bar.

The masts of the mortar schooners were dressed off with bushes so that they could not be distinguished easily from the trees along the shore; and as soon as they were moored in their chosen position the bombardment was begun. The forts could not be seen from them, and the gunners fired with a computed aim, throwing the immense shells high into the air, that they might fall almost perpendicularly into the forts and explode. The bombardment was kept up steadily for six days and nights, nearly six thousand shells being thrown. They fell in and around the fortifications, destroyed buildings, cut the levee, and killed fourteen men and wounded thirty-nine. It is said that in modern warfare a man's weight in lead is fired for every man that is killed; in this instance about sixteen tons of iron were thrown for every man that was injured. The main object, however, was not to disable the garrisons, but to dismount the guns and render the fortifications useless; and this result was not accomplished. The forts and their armaments were in almost as good condition for service as ever.

Meanwhile, Farragut had made up his mind that to anchor abreast of these fortifications and attack them would simply be to lose his vessels. It is only in its ability to keep moving that a war ship (at least a wooden one, and there was not an ironclad in this fleet) has an advantage over land works of equal armament. To surrender this advantage at the beginning is to lose the fight at the end. Furthermore, he believed that as the sole purpose of the forts was to protect the city, if he could lay the city under his guns the forts would be abandoned. Consequently, in spite of the advice of the eminent army engineer and his friend and brother officer, Porter, he determined to pass the forts with his whole fleet (except the mortar schooners) and appear before New Orleans.

This was a new thing in warfare, and it is important to note it here, because George Dewey, who had been promoted to a lieutenancy at the beginning of the war, was in that fleet, and Farragut was his instructor as well as his commander.

The passage was to be made in the night, and Farragut—who had learned to perform every duty that is ever required on shipboard, except those of the surgeon—gave in his general orders minute instructions for every preparation, and suggested that the officers and crew of each vessel add any other precautions that their ingenuity might devise.

Every man in the fleet was busy. In the forecastle of the Mississippi a group of sailors were mak-

Whitewashing the decks.

ing splinter nettings, criticising the arrangements for the attack, and speculating as to the result.

"What's Bill Ammon going to do with that white paint?" said one.

"He's going to paint the gun deck," answered a comrade.

"What! paint it white?"

"Yes, white."

"What's that for? To make us a better target for the reb gunners?"

"It's to make it so that we can see what we're about, and find things when we need them."

"That seems to say we're going up in the night," said the first speaker.

"You've hit it," said another; "that's exactly what we are in for."

"Whose idea is this of painting the decks?" asked a fourth.

"Bill pretends it's his," said the boatswain's mate. "He thinks it's a great idea. But I was by when he got his orders, and I know it originated with Dewey."

"I don't care where the idea came from," said the sailmaker. "I don't admire it."

"Why not?"

"Because it's just the wrong thing. The boys on the Pensacola and the Oneida are rubbing the decks over with mud, so that the Johnnies will have a hard time to distinguish them. I think that's the true idea."

"I can't agree with you there," said the boatswain's mate. "As soon as we get fairly into it the smoke will be so thick that the Johnnies can't see through it very perfectly anyway. And that's just when we want to see everything on our own deck."

"It may be so," grumbled the sailmaker; "but if it comes to that, old Dewey'd better have the river whitewashed, so that he can see to con the ship."

This bit of sailor wit created laughter, of which the little company were in much need, for some of them were not at all hopeful of the coming contest.

"He'll con the ship all right," said another sailor, who had not spoken before, and who answered to the nickname of Slippery Sim (his real name being Simeon Nelson). "I knew him in Montpelier, and I know you can depend on him every time."

"In Montpelier?" said the boatswain's mate. "Why, that was about Bill Ammon's latitude and longitude, if my reckoning's right."

"It was, exactly," said Nelson.

"Then he ought to have known Dewey too," said the boatswain's mate.

"Know him?" said Nelson. "I should say he did know him. The most famous of all the fights that ever took place among our boys was between him and Dewey."

"Did you see it?" said the sailmaker eagerly.

"I did," said Nelson in an impressive tone. "I had the honor of holding Ammon's coat."

"And which licked?" asked the sailmaker.

"Hold on!" said the boatswain's mate. "Don't answer that question. Never spoil a good story by telling it stern foremost. Give us the whole narratyve from beginning to end, and don't let us know which licked till you get to the very last. If those two fellows were at it, I know it must have been a tug. A good description of it ought to brace us up for the lively fight that's before us."

"Yes," said another, "it may be the last story that some of us will ever hear."

"Don't be down-hearted, Ned," said the first speaker. "I've sailed with old Farragut nearly eighteen years, and I know he'll pull us through."

"I haven't any doubt that he'll pull the fleet through all right," said Ned. "But even a victorious fleet generally has a few red spots on the decks, and not so many gunners when it comes out as when it went in. It's all right, of course. I'm not finding fault, and I'm not any more afraid than I ought to be. I expect to stand up and do my duty, as I know the rest of you will. But a man can't help being a human creature, with human feelings, if he *is* a sailor; and when he's killed he's just as much killed, and all his pretty plans spoiled, whether it's in a victory or in a defeat."

"That's all true enough, Ned," said the boatswain's mate; "but what we want to cultivate just now is the spirit of fight, not the spirit of philosophy. Save your philosophy till after the battle, and then you'll have plenty of good company, for then everybody will be philosophizing about it."

"They will, indeed," said the sailmaker, "and a good many of them will be telling how they could have managed it better that we did. The great trouble in this war is that so many of our best generals and admirals who ought to be in the field or on shipboard have jobs in barber shops that they don't like to give up, or can't be spared from country stores and newspaper offices."

"Oh, belay your sarcasm," said the boatswain's mate. "Let's have the story of the big fight between Dewey and Ammon, Sim."

Thereupon Nelson gave a minute and graphic account of that schoolboy contest.

"I don't see," said Ned, "why Bill Ammon never has mentioned that he was a schoolmate of Dewey's. I should think he would be proud of it."

"The reason is plain enough," said the sailmaker.

"He was afraid that might lead up to the story of this fight. Probably he would be quite willing that it should remain untold."

"Well, whatever he was in school days," said Ned, "Bill's a pretty good fellow now; and I don't see that he has much to be ashamed of. It seems he put up a good stiff fight then, and I think he'll do his duty with the best of us now."

"Yes, that's so!" responded two or three.

"Talking about that whitewashing," said the sailor who had opened the conversation, "I think it's all right enough, but it seems to me it might have been applied where it would have done still more good."

"Where's that, Tom?" said the boatswain's mate.

"I suppose you know," said Tom, "that the Itasca and Pinola went up last night to break the chain and make an opening for the fleet to pass through. Caldwell did that all right. But it's going to be a mighty hard matter to steer these big sea-going vessels through that narrow place in the current of a river like this and in the smoke of battle. The thing I'm most afraid of is that some one of our ships will get tangled up among those hulks, and then the rebs can just pound her as if they had her in a mortar. Suppose the ship at the head of the line should get caught across the opening, where would the whole fleet be then?"

"Of course there is great risk," said the boatswain's mate, "but how are you going to avoid it? They took up a new-fangled torpedo to blow up some of the hulks and make a wider opening, but the thing wouldn't work. Those machines that are to go off under water seldom do work."

"I was thinking," said Tom, "that if they had whitewashed the decks of the hulks next to the opening it would go far to prevent such an accident."

"You didn't go up there with Caldwell, and neither did your brother," said the sailmaker. "If you had, I don't think you'd have been anxious to whitewash anything and make yourselves a better target for the sharpshooters on shore. Our men were fired on all the while as it was."

"I think I could have managed it," said Tom.

"Tell us how."

"I would have taken up some buckets of white paint—I see you smile, but you've got ahead of your reckoning. No, I wasn't going to say I'd take some brushes along and make a nice job painting the decks. I'd keep the buckets covered up till just as we were ready to come away, and then I'd simply overturn them on the decks and push off. That would whiten them enough to help our pilots through."

"I'm not sure but that's a good idea," said another sailor.

"Is it?" said the boatswain's mate. "I guess you've never sailed with Caldwell or Dewey. If you had you'd know that either of them would be more horrified at the idea of any such sloppy work, even on the deck of an old hulk, than at doubling the risk of his ship. They're dandies, both of 'em."

"If anything gets afoul of the hulks," remarked a sailor who had not spoken before, "it will probably be this old spinning wheel. The Secretary of the Navy that ordered a side-wheeler for a war ship must have been born and brought up in the backwoods. If we could have got the Colorado over the bar I wouldn't be here. She's the ship we ought to have if we're going to knock those forts to pieces."

"I'm not sure that the largest ships are the best for this work," said the sailmaker. "This whole fleet was built for sea service, and it's out of place in a river like this."

"Of course it's a loss not to have the Colorado with us," said the boatswain's mate. "But the best thing that was aboard of her *is* with us."

"What's that?" said several.

"That old sea dog Bailey," answered the boatswain's mate. "He's no dandy, but he knows what to do with a ship in a fight or in a storm or anywhere else. I was with him on the Lexington in forty-six, when we went round Cape Horn to California. That was the beginning of the Mexican War. We carried troops and army officers. Bill Sherman, who commanded a brigade at Bull Run, was among them. So was General Halleck—he was only a lieutenant then."

"Bailey's on the Cayuga now," said the sailor from the Colorado, "and if Farragut understands his business he'll let him lead the line, unless Farragut leads it himself in the flagship. I wish I could be with him; but when we had to leave the Colorado outside they scattered our crew all through the fleet, and I just had the luck to be sent to this old coffee mill."

"As long as Doc. Dewey's on the bridge you needn't be afraid of her," said Sim Nelson, "whether she's a spinning wheel or a coffee mill—and your opinion seems to vary on that point. There was lots of good fighting before propellers were invented, but you appear to think we can't do anything without a propeller."

"A propeller isn't very likely to be struck by a shot," said the man from the Colorado; "but these old windmill sails going round on each side of this tub can hardly help being hit."

"Now you just quit worrying, and settle your mind on an even keel," said Sim Nelson. "There's such a thing as ability, and there's such a thing as luck. Ability and luck don't always go together—more's the pity! There's McDowell at Bull Run, as able as any general there, and he planned the battle well, and our boys put up a good stiff fight; but just at the last the luck turned against him, and then where was he? 'Tisn't so with Doc. Dewey. I've known him ever since we were boys, and his ability and luck always went together. I've no doubt there are plenty of good officers in the fleet, but I'm glad to have him on the bridge of the ship that I sail in, whether it's an old spinning wheel, or a coffee mill, or a windmill, or whatever other name you may invent for it."

The man from the Colorado said no more, and a few minutes later the boatswain called away half of the men who were making netting to assist in protecting the boilers and machinery. They piled up hammocks and coal in such a way as to stop a good many shots that might otherwise reach these vital parts of the ship.

They had not quite finished this task when there was a cry of "Fire raft!" followed quickly by an order to man two boats. Hardly any time seemed to elapse before the boats swung down from the davits and the oarsmen pulled away with a strong, steady stroke. In the stern of each stood two men with a long pole, on the end of which was an iron hook.

Up the stream a little way was an immense mass of flame, gliding down with the current. In the center it was crackling, at the side occasionally hissing where a burning stick touched the water, and above it rose a dense column of smoke, curved at the top and swaying in the light breeze.

"That's the fifth of those villainous valentines they've sent us," said the man from the Colorado.

"Well, we took good care of the other four," said the boatswain, "and I guess we can take care of this, though it's the biggest and ugliest of all. It won't be long now before we send 'em the answer, post paid. Back water, there! back water!"

This command was uttered and obeyed none too quickly. Two of the gunboats—the Kineo and the Sciota—trying to avoid the fire raft, collided violently, and the mainmast of the Sciota went overboard with a crash and just missed striking the boat. Then both the gunboats dragged across the bows of the Mississippi, but skillful management prevented any further damage there, and the two small boats pulled up close to the windward side of the fire raft, at the same time with four boats from two other ships. The men in the stern struck their hooks into the side of the flatboat that formed the base of the blazing pile, and the oarsmen pulled for the shore. The heat almost shriveled the skin on their faces, but they bent to the work with a will, and slowly towed the monster away from the line of the fleet, down stream more than two miles, and then over to the western bank, where they pushed it into the shallow water and mud and left it to burn itself away, a beautiful and harmless spectacle.

As they pulled back to their ships they noticed that the various crews were at work "stopping" the sheet cables up and down the sides, in the line of the engines.

"That's a splendid idea; whose is it?" asked the man at the stroke oar.

"Yes," said the boatswain, "it makes them iron-clad as far as it goes. They say it was suggested by Engineer Moore, of the Richmond."

"Splendid fellow!" said the man from the Colorado. "He was a schoolmate of mine."

"Where was that?" said the boatswain.

"Detroit," said the man from the Colorado. "He and I used to run away from school together and swim across to Windsor."

"Um—about half a mile," said the boatswain, musingly, "and current eight miles an hour—very good swimming for boys. But," he added aloud, "Mr. Moore ought to know about that. He thinks he was born and brought up in Plattsburg, New York— I heard him say so—and that his father was in the battle of Lake Champlain. What funny mistakes men make about themselves sometimes!"

The man from the Colorado said no more.

Two o'clock in the morning of April 24, 1862, was fixed as the hour for the fleet to weigh anchor and steam up the river. The moon would rise an hour and a half later, and it was the intention to pass the forts in darkness and have the benefit of moonlight after the gauntlet had been run. Five minutes before two the signal was given—two red lights at the masthead of the flagship; but it was moonrise before all were ready and in motion. The question of a moon, however, was no longer of any consequence, for the Confederates had observed the preparations, and had set fire to immense piles of wood that they kept for the purpose at the ends of the chain, so that the whole scene was as light as day. This did not stop Farragut, who had made up his mind to pass the forts and lay the city under his guns.

The mortar schooners moved up stream to a point near Fort Jackson, and began a heavy bombardment. Then the fleet, in a long line, steamed steadily up the river, passed through the opening in the chain, and with rapid broadsides swept the bastions of the forts as they went by. It was in three divisions. The first, consisting of eight vessels, was led by Captain Theodorus Bailey in the Cayuga; the second, of

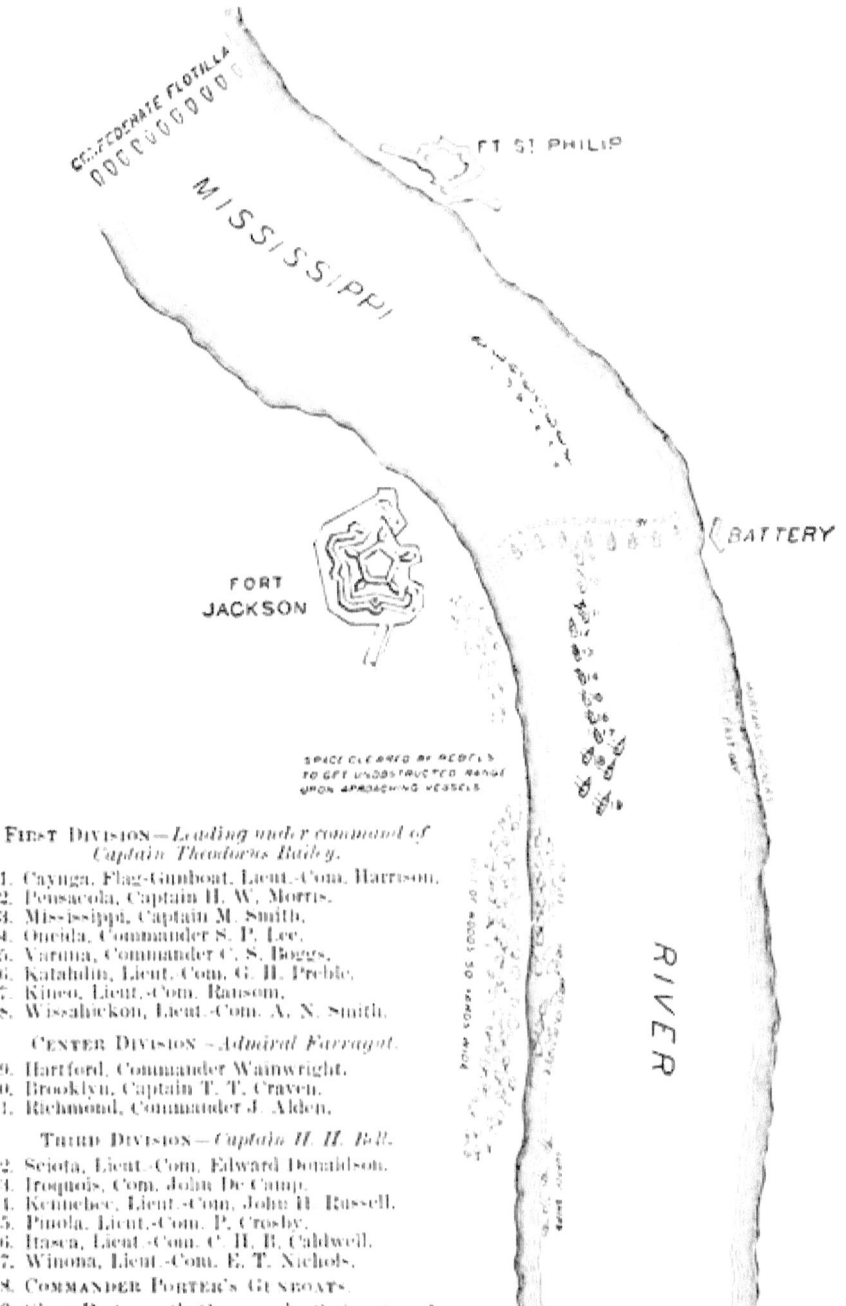

Order of attack on Forts Jackson and St. Philip.

three vessels, by Farragut in the Hartford; and the third, of six vessels, by Captain Henry H. Bell in the Sciota.

Following the gunboat Cayuga in the first division was the sloop-of-war Pensacola; and next came the side-wheel steamer Mississippi, commanded by Captain Melancton Smith. Her conning bridge rested with its ends on the tops of the high paddle-boxes, and Lieutenant George Dewey, the executive officer, was stationed there to direct her course.

When the signal was given to go ahead Captain Smith asked, a little anxiously, "Do you know the channel, sir?"

"Yes, sir," answered Dewey.

The question was repeated at intervals, and every time it received the same confident answer. The lieutenant afterward admitted that his knowledge of the channel was gained by study of a chart, which was supplemented by his confidence that he could tell from the appearance of the water. Here his usual luck stood him in good stead, as the sailor in the forecastle had declared.

As soon as the Cayuga had passed through the opening in the chain, both forts began to fire on her. Within a few minutes she was pouring a sheet of grape and canister across Fort St. Philip, but she did not slacken her pace, and in ten minutes more was engaged with the Confederate fleet that was waiting for her up the stream.

The Pensacola, next in line, steamed steadily but slowly by, firing with perfect regularity, and doing specially fine execution with a rifled eighty-pounder and an eleven-inch pivot gun. But she paid for her deliberation, as her loss—thirty-seven men—was the greatest in the fleet.

Then came the Mississippi—the old spinning wheel, coffee mill, windmill, as the discontented sailor called her. By this time the air was so thick with smoke from the guns, bonfires, and fire rafts that it was only by the flashes that the gunners could see where to aim. The Mississippi went by the forts in good style, pouring in her fire as she passed, and suffering but slight loss from them. But immediately afterward, like the two vessels that had preceded her, she encountered the Confederate fleet, which consisted of the ironclad ram Manassas, the unfinished ironclad floating battery Louisiana, and a dozen gunboats, some of which were fitted to be used as rams. The Manassas drove straight at the Mississippi, with intention to sink her, and would have done so had not Dewey ordered a quick shift of the helm, which changed the direct blow into a slanting one. This, indeed, gave her a severe cut on the port quarter, and disabled some of her machinery; but at the same moment the

Mississippi poured a tremendous fire into the ram. Then she found herself in the thick of the fight with the Confederate fleet. The Oneida and the Varuna came close after her, and here was the most desperate encounter. Shells, round shot, and canister were exchanged as rapidly as the guns could be handled, some of which tore through the sides and found their way to the interior, there to break the machinery or burst and scatter death, while some swept along the decks and struck down the men at the guns. In an action like that the men are under the greatest excitement, with every muscle tense and every nerve strained; and when a ball strikes one it shivers him as if he were made of glass, and scatters ghastly fragments over his comrades. In the confined space where the men work the guns, and with the smoke of battle enveloping them, there is no opportunity to dodge the shot or know they are coming before they have done their work. The only defense consists in rapid and accurate firing by the men, with skill and quick judgment on the part of him who directs the movements of the ship. Everything was ablaze, and the roar was terrific, when a great shot bounced in at one of the ports of the Mississippi, knocked over a gun, killed one gunner and wounded three others, and passed out on the other side. Almost at the same moment the ship from which it was fired received a discharge from the Mississippi that swept away a whole gun's crew. Then there were rapid maneuvers, to ram or avoid ramming, rake or avoid raking, and all the while the guns were booming, shot and splinters were flying across the decks, man after man was struck down, and blood ran out at the scuppers. Signal men in the rigging, sailors with howitzers and muskets in the tops, officers on the bridges, gunners between decks, engineers, firemen, and surgeons below—all were in a state of intense action. The largest of the Confederate vessels, a powerful steamer fitted as a ram, attacked the Varuna, and was subjected to a murderous raking fire from that ship. Finding that his bow gun was mounted too far aft to strike her when at such close quarters, the Confederate commander depressed it and fired through the bow of his own vessel. Then another ram came up and joined in the attack, and the Varuna was reduced to a wreck and driven ashore.

Meanwhile, the second division of the fleet came up, led by the Hartford. This vessel, in attempting to avoid a fire raft, struck on a shoal; then the ram Manassas pushed another blazing raft against her quarter, and in a moment she was on fire. The great excitement thus produced on board the flagship did not for a moment interfere with the discipline. A part of her crew were called to fire quarters and

THE FIGHT FOR NEW ORLEANS.

put out the flames, while the rest continued to work the guns with perfect regularity. Then she was backed off into deep water, and continued up stream, firing into every enemy she could reach. A steamer loaded with men (probably intended as a boarding party) bore down upon the flagship, but the marines promptly fired a shell into her which exploded, and she disappeared.

While the Mississippi was engaged in this desperate battle an officer on board kept his eye on Lieutenant Dewey—for on him every movement of the ship depended—and he has described the figure of the young officer on the high bridge as it was alternately hidden by the smoke and illuminated by the flashes of the artillery.

"Every time the dark came back," he says, "I felt sure that we never should see Dewey again. His cap was blown off, and his eyes were aflame; but he gave his orders with the air of a man in thorough command of himself."

The ram Manassas, after her encounter with the Mississippi, had passed down the river in pursuit of other prey, and delivered a blow at the Brooklyn which failed to sink her only because she was promptly turned so as not to receive it at right angles. Then the ram was discovered coming up stream, and Captain Smith signaled to the flagship for permission to attack her with the Mississippi. This being promptly granted, the brave old side-wheeler swung about in the stream and went straight for her dangerous enemy. She failed in an attempt to run down the ram, but crippled it and drove it ashore, when the crew were seen to come out at the little hatch, jump to the levee, and disappear in the swamp. The Mississippi then poured into her another broadside, and she drifted down the stream and blew up.

Fourteen of Farragut's seventeen vessels had succeeded in passing the obstructions and participating in the battle. One of these, the Varuna, was destroyed. All the others carried the scars of battle, and all save one had casualties on board, varying in number from thirty-seven on the Pensacola, thirty-five on the Brooklyn, and twenty-eight on the Iroquois, to a single one on the Portsmouth. The Mississippi lost two men killed and six wounded. The total loss in the fleet was thirty-seven men killed and a hundred and forty-seven wounded. On the other hand, the Confederate fleet was destroyed, the last vessel afloat—the ironclad Louisiana—being blown up by her commander three days later; and the next day after that a land force commanded by General Butler came up in rear of the forts, and they were surrendered.

When the dead were laid out side by side on the

decks for the last rites, there were manly tears on the faces of many of their shipmates, and the eyes of dear old Farragut were not dry.

The larger part of the fleet pushed on up the river, and the next day the city of New Orleans was captured.

No such battle as this had been seen before, and no such ever will be seen again. A fleet of wooden vessels, all built for sea service, had entered a river and fought against obstructions, fire rafts, fortifications, rams, ironclads, and gunboats, and had won a complete victory over all. This was a wonderful school for a young officer.

CHAPTER VIII.

THE BATTLE AT PORT HUDSON.

NEW ORLEANS being captured and firmly held, the next problem was to patrol and police the Mississippi from that point to Cairo, Illinois, and prevent the Confederates from crossing it with troops and supplies. Thus only could the full fruits of Farragut's original and brilliant exploit be secured. As soon as the war was fairly begun, the Government had ordered an ironclad fleet of light draught to be built for service on the Western rivers, and many of these vessels were completed in a hundred days from the laying of the keel. They took pretty good care of the river above Vicksburg, and below that point Farragut's fleet was expected to do the work. This was an arduous and monotonous task, calling for patience, endurance, and skill, involving almost daily loss of single lives from field artillery and sharpshooters on shore, but giving few opportunities for glory.

At two points, both on the eastern side of the river, the Confederates constructed formidable works, with heavy artillery. These were Vicksburg and Port Hudson, about a hundred miles apart. The choice of these points was for a double reason. At each of them a line of transportation from the southwest reached the river, by which supplies were brought for the Confederate armies in the States farther east; and at each of them there was a bend in the stream, with high bluffs on the eastern side and low land on the western. Thus the two points that it was most desirable to protect were most easily protected.

General Butler was superseded in command at New Orleans by General Banks; and after a time it was planned that Banks should move up with a large force to attack Port Hudson, while an army under General Grant came from above to capture Vicksburg; and the fleets were expected to assist in both of these campaigns.

Great difficulties were met by the national armies, and everything appeared to move with insufferable slowness. The authorities at Washington seemed to think that as Farragut's fleet had passed the batteries below New Orleans, it could pass any batteries, and a spirit of impatience was manifest because the river was not quickly and thoroughly cleared and held. A very important difference in the circumstances was overlooked. The forts below New Orleans were on low ground, and as the fleet sailed by, its decks were nearly or quite on a level with the bastions, which could be swept by the fire of the broadsides. But at Vicksburg and Port Hudson the batteries were on high bluffs and could send down a plunging fire on the ships, to which the fleet could hardly reply with much effect.

Finally, the Admiral received peremptory orders to "clear the river through," which meant, run by the fortifications of Vicksburg and capture or destroy the Confederate vessels above that point that were either afloat or being built. The most important of these was the powerful ironclad ram Arkansas, which was expected to come out of the Arkansas or the Yazoo River into the Mississippi and attack the fleet of gunboats.

Farragut had appeared before Vicksburg in May and demanded the surrender of the place; but this was refused, and without the co-operation of an army the demand could not be enforced. The construction of the defenses then proceeded more rapidly than before, and when his peremptory orders came, late in June, the place was very strong. On the 28th he attempted the passage with ten vessels, aided by the mortar flotilla. While the mortars were raining shells into the works the vessels steamed up the river in two columns, and all passed the batteries except three of the rear division, which, from a misunderstanding

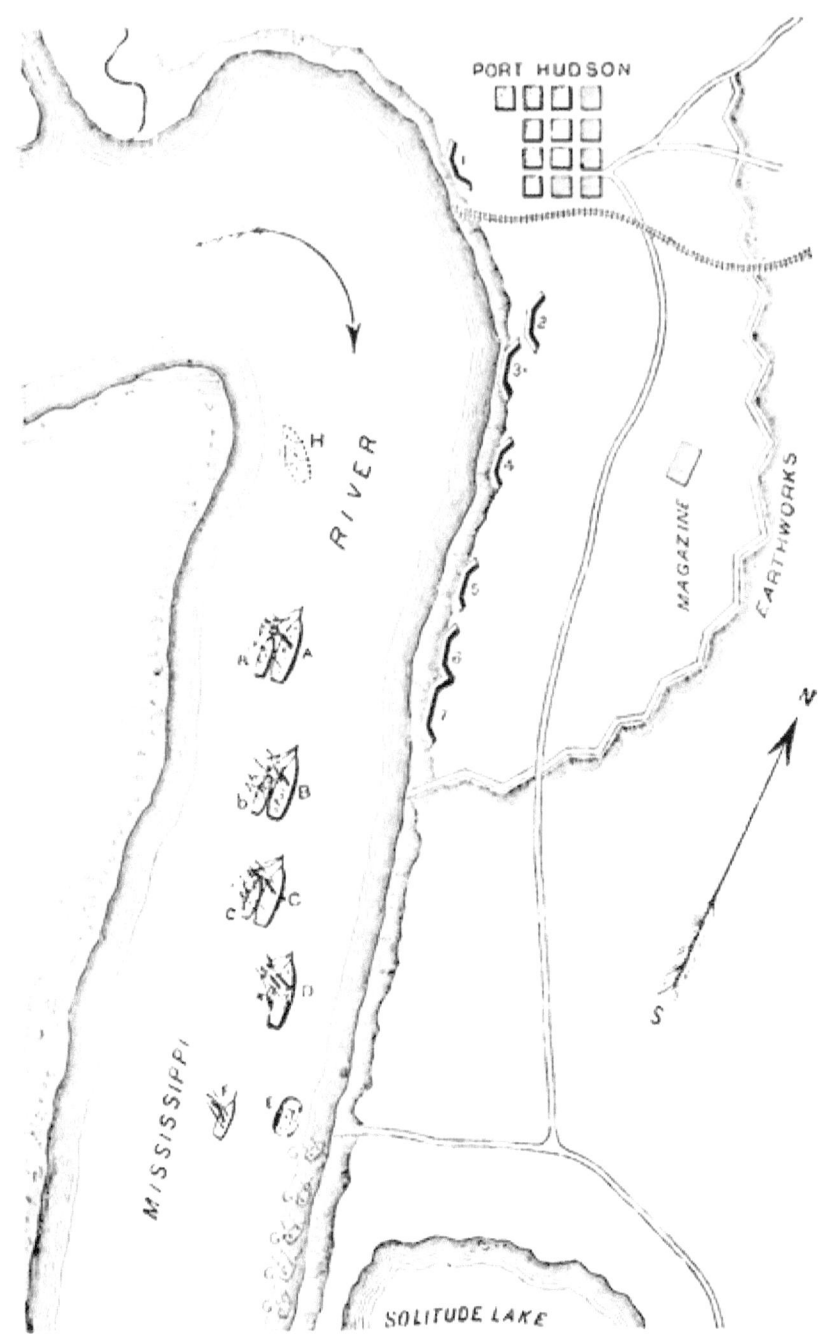

Order of attack on Port Hudson.

A. Hartford (flag ship), Captain James S. Palmer. a. Albatross, Lieut.-Com. John E. Hart. B. Richmond, Commander James Alden. b. Genesee, Commander W. H. Macomb. C. Monongahela, Captain J. P. McKinstry. c. Kineo, Lieut.-Com. John Waters. D. Mississippi, Captain Melancton Smith. E. Essex, Commander C. H. B. Caldwell. F. Sachem, Act. Vol. Lieut. Amos Johnson. G. G. Mortar schooners. H. Spot where Mississippi grounded.

of orders, fell back. The losses in the fleet were fifteen men killed and forty wounded. One gunboat received a shot through the boiler, which killed six men by scalding. No other vessel was seriously injured.

Dewey's ship, the Mississippi, did not participate in this exploit. The affair has been described briefly here because of its influence on a later and more hazardous one in which she did take part, to her cost. The passage of the Vicksburg batteries convinced the men of the navy that, with small loss, they could pass any batteries, no matter how situated. Farragut wrote: "The Department will perceive from my report that the forts can be passed, and we have done it, and can do it again as often as it may be required of us."

That was in the summer of 1862, when Vicksburg was but partially fortified and Port Hudson hardly at all. But the Confederate Government awoke to the extreme importance of those points, and the work of fortifying them went on rapidly. In some respects the fortifications of Port Hudson, on the river side at least, were even more formidable than those of Vicksburg. After a reconnoissance in the autumn of 1862, Commander Lowry reported: "The plan appears to be this: to place their works in such a position that, we having passed or silenced one or more of the lower batteries, other concealed batteries open, which will throw a cross fire into the stern of the vessels, which would then be exposed to a cross fire from batteries yet to be approached and silenced and from the masked ones left astern."

In March, 1863, it was arranged that Farragut should run by the batteries of Port Hudson, while Banks, with twelve thousand men, should assail them on the land side. The objects to be gained by running by the batteries were: To concentrate the fleet above Port Hudson for the destruction of the Confederate vessels; to blockade Red River and the bayous; and to communicate with the naval and military forces that were besieging Vicksburg.

On the 14th Farragut completed his preparations, and that night was selected as the time for the movement. His fleet consisted of four ships and three gunboats, besides the mortar schooners and their attendant gunboats. Each of the ships, except the Mississippi, was to have a gunboat lashed to its port side, so that if one were disabled its gunboat could tow it through or out of the fight. The Mississippi could not take a gunboat, because she was a side-wheeler. All the vessels were trimmed by the head, so that if one grounded it would strike bow first and would not be swung round by the current. And the elaborate precautions that had been taken below New

THE BATTLE AT PORT HUDSON. 97

Orleans were repeated. The order of the column was this:

> The flagship Hartford, with the gunboat Albatross.
> The Richmond, with the gunboat Genesee.
> The Monongahela, with the gunboat Kineo.
> The Mississippi.

The "old spinning wheel" was still commanded by Captain Melancton Smith, with Lieutenant Dewey as his executive officer, as when she participated in the capture of New Orleans.

At Port Hudson there is a sharp bend in the river, and the deep channel runs close under the bluffs of the eastern bank, while the water shoals off to the low western shore. At dusk the signal was displayed for the fleet to form in line and follow the flagship. This was a red lantern hung out over the stern of the Hartford. The order was quietly and promptly obeyed. Like every officer in the fleet, Lieutenant George Dewey was at his post and eager for the adventure. His post now, as before, was on the bridge, to direct the course of the ship.

Every man on board was alert. The splinter nettings were on, and the carpenters were ready to stop shot holes or repair other damage. The marines had their muskets in hand to repel boarders. One officer was making sure that all was in shape for "fire quarters" if that order should be sounded, and another was looking to the rifled gun. The men at the great guns stood with their sleeves rolled up for instant work.

The darkness closed in rapidly, and the night was absolutely calm. The Hartford slowly steamed ahead, and the other ships took their places in the line.

But with all possible quietness of preparation the vigilant Confederates were not to be deceived or surprised. Hardly was the fleet under way when two rockets rose into the air from the right bank of the river, and then the first of the shore batteries discharged its guns. At the same time several great bonfires were lighted, and then everything on the river was in plain sight until the battle had gone on long enough to produce a great pall of cannon smoke. The other shore batteries opened in rapid succession, and the mortar schooners promptly began their work. The great thirteen-inch shells, with their burning fuses, rose in beautiful curves and passed overhead like meteors, to fall and explode within and around the fortifications. As the several ships came within reach of the enemy they opened fire, and in a little time the smoke was so thick that the gunners could only aim at the flashes. But they forged ahead steadily, doing their best under a terrific fire from the batteries on the bluff and the constant rifle practice of sharpshooters on the western bank. The Hartford and her

Passage of the batteries of Port Hudson.

gunboat got by, losing only one man killed and two wounded; but, though she had two of the most skillful pilots, she grounded directly under the enemy's guns, and for a little while was in danger of destruction. By skillful handling of the gunboat she was backed off, and then continued up stream beyond the range of fire. The Admiral now looked for his other vessels, and they were nowhere to be seen.

The Richmond, which had almost run into the Hartford when she grounded, had reached the last battery, and in a few minutes would have been beyond the reach of its guns, when a shot struck her steam pipe near the safety valves and disabled her. The gunboat was not able to take her farther against the strong current, and they were obliged to drop down stream out of the fight. They had lost three men killed and twelve wounded. A cannon shot took off the leg of the executive officer, and he died a few days later. An attempt was made to blow her up with a torpedo, but at the moment of explosion, though it shattered the cabin windows, it was not quite near enough to do serious damage.

The Monongahela grounded on the western shore near the bend of the river, and for half an hour was exposed to a merciless fire. The rudder of her gunboat had been rendered useless, and then a shot wrecked the bridge of the Monongahela, throwing

Captain McKinstry to the deck and disabling him, and, passing on, killed three men. Though shots were constantly striking her, and had dismounted three of her guns, perfect coolness was maintained by the officers, with discipline on the part of the crew. The gunboat was shifted to the other side of the ship, and presently she was pulled off into deep water and resumed her course up stream, firing shells and shrapnel into the fortifications. She had almost passed the principal battery when the crank pin of her engine became heated, and she could go no farther. Then she also was obliged to run down with the current out of range. She had lost six men killed and twenty-one wounded.

While Farragut was anxiously looking down stream in hope to see the approach of his missing fleet, suddenly a great light shot up into the sky, and the man at the masthead reported that a ship was on fire.

The Mississippi, like the other vessels, had followed steadily after the flagship, feeling her way amid the smoke and rapidly firing her starboard guns, when she, like the other ships, grounded at the turn and "heeled over three streaks to port." The engine was at once reversed, the port guns were run in, and the pressure of steam was increased to the greatest amount that the boilers would bear, but all in vain—

she could not move herself off and she had no gunboat to assist.

Meanwhile, three batteries had got her range, and under this terrible cross fire she was hulled at every discharge. Her starboard guns were still worked regularly and as rapidly as possible, to diminish the enemy's fire. Then in quick succession came the commands from Captain Smith:

"Spike the port battery and throw it overboard!"

"Spike the pivot gun and throw it overboard!"

"Bring up the sick and the wounded!"

The spiking was done by the hands of Lieutenant Dewey, Ensign Bachelder, and Assistant-Engineer Tower, but there was no time to throw the guns overboard.

Every man in the ship knew the meaning of these preparations for abandoning her.

Captain Smith was determined that, as he must lose his vessel, nothing should be left of it for the enemy. While he was lighting a cigar he said to Dewey:

"It is not likely that we shall escape, and we must make every preparation to insure the destruction of the ship."

The crew were ordered to throw the small arms overboard, and the engineers to destroy the engine. Then fire was set in the forward storeroom, but very soon three shots that penetrated the side below the line let in enough water to extinguish it. After that she was fired in four places. She had been struck by the enemy's shot two hundred and fifty times.

There were but three small boats, and these were used first to take away the sick and the wounded. At no time was the least confusion or disorder apparent among the crew; but when they saw how rapidly the old ship was approaching destruction, and how limited were the means of safety, some of them jumped overboard and swam for the shore, and these were fired at by sharpshooters on the bank. Dewey, noticing that one of them, a strong swimmer, suddenly became almost helpless, guessed that he had been struck by a bullet. As the lieutenant then had little to do but wait for the return of the boat, he plunged into the stream, struck out for the disabled sailor, and very soon was near enough to recognize him.

"Hello! is that you, Bill Ammon?" said Dewey.

"It is, sir," said Bill, not even in his agony forgetting the etiquette of shipboard.

"What has happened to you?"

"A musket ball in the shoulder, sir."

The lieutenant had now reached him, and with one arm sustained him while he swam slowly to a broken spar that fortunately was afloat at a little distance. Finding that his old schoolmate had strength enough to cling to this till he should be picked up (for the Essex had now come up to assist, and her boats were out), Dewey swam back to the ship.

When all had been taken off except the captain and the executive officer, who were standing on the quarter-deck, Captain Smith said:

"Are you sure she will burn to the water?"

"I will go down and make sure," Dewey answered; and down he went into the wardroom, at the risk of his life, and saw that everything was ablaze.

When he returned to the deck and reported, the captain was satisfied, and then the two officers left in the last boat and passed down to the Richmond under the fire of the batteries.

When the flames had sufficiently lightened the Mississippi she floated off, swung round into the current, and drifted down stream, bow foremost.

The port battery, which had been loaded but not fired, now went off, sending its shot toward the enemy, as if the old craft knew herself and wanted to do her duty to the last. At half past five o'clock in the morning the fire reached her magazine, and the terrific explosion that followed not only blew the vessel to fragments, but was heard and felt at a distance of several miles. She had lost sixty-four of her crew, some of whom were killed by shot, some drowned, and some made prisoners when they swam ashore.

Removing the wounded

CHAPTER IX.

THE CAPTURE OF FORT FISHER.

THE port of Wilmington, North Carolina, on Cape Fear River, about twenty miles from its mouth, was one of the most difficult to blockade, and when the other ports of the Southern States had been closed one after another, this became the Confederacy's main reliance for such supplies as had to be imported. Hence the desire of the national administration and military authorities to seal it up. This could be done only by capturing its defenses, and the principal of these was Fort Fisher, the strongest earthwork then in existence. This fortification, with its outworks, occupied the end of the narrow peninsula between Cape Fear River and the ocean. It mounted thirty-eight heavy guns; the parapets were twenty-five feet thick and twenty feet high; there were heavy traverses, bombproofed; ditches and palisades surrounded it; and outside of these were buried torpedoes connected with electric batteries in the casemates. The garrison consisted of about two thousand men.

In December, 1864, it was proposed to capture

this work by a combined land and naval force. The troops sent for the purpose were commanded by General Butler. The fleet was the largest that ever had been gathered under the American flag, and was commanded by Rear-Admiral David D. Porter. It consisted of fifty-six wooden vessels and four ironclads. The Colorado, commanded by Captain Henry K. Thatcher, was one of the largest wooden ships; she was the one that could not be taken over the bar to participate in the attack on the forts below New Orleans. Her place in this battle was second ship in second division.

Lieutenant George Dewey, after his experience on the Mississippi, had served for a time in the James River flotilla under Commander McComb, and then was ordered to the Colorado, in which he participated in both attacks on Fort Fisher.

An accidental explosion of a boat load of powder, a short time before, which produced a concussion that shook down buildings, suggested the possibility of damaging the fort by similar means, and it was resolved to try the experiment. An old steamer filled with powder and disguised as a blockade runner was taken in close to the fort in the night of December 23d and exploded within three hundred yards of the beach. But no effect whatever was produced upon the fort or its equipment.

The next day two thirds of the fleet—the remainder being held in reserve—steamed slowly in, anchored in their appointed order, and began a bombardment, directing their fire principally at the guns of the fort. This was kept up all day, and there was such a play of bursting shells over and within the works as never had been seen before. Two magazines were exploded, and several buildings were burned. The fire was returned by the fort, and some vessels were injured by the shells, but no casualties resulted from it except by the explosion of a shell in the boiler of the Mackinaw. There were serious casualties in the fleet, however, from the bursting of hundred-pounder rifled guns. There were four of these accidents, by which fifteen men were killed and twenty-two wounded.

The next day, which was Christmas, the troops were landed from the transports, and the fleet renewed the bombardment in the expectation that the troops would be marched to the rear of the fort and storm it. But General Butler and General Weitzel made a reconnoissance, and agreed that the works could not be carried by assault. They therefore re-embarked the troops and steamed back to Fort Monroe. In the two days the fleet had fired fifteen thousand shells, and disabled nine guns in the fort.

This fiasco was a disappointment and mortification to the President and General Grant, who believed they had furnished a force to which they had a right to look for substantial results. They therefore resolved upon a second attempt, and this time the command of the troops was intrusted to General Alfred H. Terry. Porter's fleet renewed its supplies of coal and ammunition, and at the same time kept up a moderate fire on the fort to prevent repair of the works or erection of new ones.

Terry's transports arrived the first week in January, in the midst of a heavy storm. But the vessels rode it out safely, and then preparations were made for an early assault. On the 13th the fleet anchored as near the fort as the depth of water would permit, in the same order as before, and bombarded nearly all day while the troops were debarking. A curious incident occurred when they shelled the woods back of the fort; several hundred cattle there, intended for the garrison, were frightened by the bursting shells and rushed down to the beach, where Terry's men secured them.

Admiral Ammen, who commanded the Mohican in the first division, says: "As the sun went down and the shadows fell over the waters, the spectacle was truly grand; the smoke rose and partially drifted off, permitting glimpses now and then of the earthwork, and the fitful yet incessant gleams from the hundreds of shells bursting on or beyond the parapet illuminated, like lightning flashes, the clouds above and the smoke of battle beneath."

General Terry gave his troops a day to rest, get over the effects of the sea voyage, and throw up intrenchments across the peninsula two miles above the fort. The 15th was fixed upon for the grand assault, and the entire fleet had orders to move up and bombard at an early hour. Admiral Porter thought to assist the army further by detailing sixteen hundred sailors and four hundred marines to land on the beach and assail the sea face of the fort while the army stormed the land side. The sailors were armed with cutlasses and revolvers, and looked upon this new service as a sort of lark, but they found it a serious matter before the day was over. They came in several detachments, from different ships, and, never having been drilled together for any task of this kind, did not know how to work together. But, even if they had, it is doubtful if they could have accomplished anything; for, though they sprang to the assault nimbly enough, a large part of the garrison were called to that side of the work to repel them, and before they could get near enough to use their pistols their ranks were so thinned by grape shot and musketry that they were compelled to fall back and seek shelter. Three times they were rallied by their officers, and once they got within fifty yards of the parapet; but the murderous fire from a dense mass of soldiers behind it was too much for them. Four of their officers were killed and fifteen were wounded, while the number of sailors killed or wounded was about three hundred.

But though this assault by the sailors and marines was a failure in itself, it assisted the work of capture by calling a considerable part of the garrison to the sea face while the army assailed the rear of the fort. And the bombardment by the fleet was much more effective than in the first battle. Colonel Lamb, who commanded the fort, says: " In the former bombardment the fire of the fleet had been diffuse, but now it was concentrated and the definite object was the destruction of the land defenses by enfilade and direct fire. All day and night of the 13th and 14th the navy continued its ceaseless torment; it was impossible to repair damages at night on the land face. The Ironsides and the monitors howled their eleven and fifteen-inch shells along the parapet, scattering shrapnel in the darkness. We could scarcely gather up and bury our dead without fresh casualties. At least two hundred had been killed and wounded in the two days since the fight began."

In those three days the fleet fired nearly twenty-two thousand shells. Terry's troops worked up to positions near the fort, and on the 15th, when the fleet gave the signal for assault by blowing the steam whistles, rushed to the work. In spite of all obstructions, they gained the parapet; but this was only the beginning of the task, for the work was provided with heavy traverses, and the defenders had to be driven from one to another of these, fighting obstinately all the way, until the last was reached and surrender could no longer be avoided. The assailants had lost about seven hundred men, killed or wounded. When Fort Fisher fell, the minor defenses at the mouth of the Cape Fear fell with it, and the port of Wilmington was closed. General Lee, then besieged at Petersburg by Grant, had sent word to its commander that Fort Fisher must be held or he could not subsist his army.

Thus the young officer on the Colorado, who was to become the Hero of Manila thirty-three years later, participating in this great conflict and the resulting victory, received one more lesson in the terrible art of war.

CHAPTER X.

IN TIME OF PEACE.

COMMODORE THATCHER, in his report of the attacks on Fort Fisher, paid the highest compliment to Lieutenant Dewey, and that officer, for his meritorious services in those actions, was promoted to the rank of Lieutenant Commander. The next year (1866) he was sent to the European station, on the Kearsarge, the famous ship that fought a duel with the Alabama one Sunday in June, 1864, off the harbor of Cherbourg, and sent her antagonist to the bottom.

Early in 1867 he was ordered to duty at the Portsmouth (New Hampshire) navy yard; and in that city he met Miss Susie Goodwin, daughter of Ichabod Goodwin, the "War Governor" of New Hampshire. In the autumn of that year Commander Dewey and Miss Goodwin were married.

After service in the Colorado, the flagship of the European squadron, he was detailed as an instructor at the Naval Academy, where he spent two years. In 1872 Mrs. Dewey died in Newport, and the same year he was made commander of the Narragansett and sent to the Pacific Coast Survey, on which he spent four years. Then he was lighthouse inspector and secretary of the Lighthouse Board till 1882, when he was assigned to the command of the Juniata in the Asiatic squadron. The fact that he spent two years there was probably one of the reasons that caused the administration to choose him for a much more important mission in those waters sixteen years later. In 1884 he received his commission as captain and was assigned to the command of the Dolphin. This was a new steel vessel, one of the four that formed the original "White Squadron," marking a significant turning-point in naval architecture.

The next year Captain Dewey was in command of the Pensacola, flagship of the European squadron; and in 1889 he was promoted to the rank of commodore and made chief of the Bureau of Equipment and Recruiting at Washington. In 1893 he became a member of the Lighthouse Board, and in 1896 President of the Board of Inspection and Survey.

Such is the record of an eminent naval officer in time of peace. But though the record is brief and makes a very simple story, the services that it represents were long and important. From the firing of the last gun in the civil war to the first in the war with Spain, a period of thirty-three years—the life of a generation—had elapsed. In that interval naval architecture, naval gunnery, and naval tactics underwent a greater change than any that they had seen since the days of Antony and Cleopatra. If George Dewey had stepped out of the naval service when the smoke rolled away after the battle of Fort Fisher, in 1865, he could not have been the man to win a victory that astonished the world in 1898. The maxim " In time of peace prepare for war " never was better observed than by the United States Government in its construction and treatment of the new navy in the eighties and the nineties; and it recognized the vital point when it secured the highest possible development of gun power by furnishing the man behind the gun with plenty of ammunition, however costly, for constant target practice, and established prizes for good shots. The idea of a modern torpedo boat darting at a great cruiser and with one charge of a high explosive sending her to the bottom is a terror, but the terror is transferred to the other deck when the torpedo boat finds herself met with a shower of balls, every one having great penetrating power and aimed with deadly precision. It is said that the credit for the system of target practice belongs primarily to Dewey's classmate and lifelong friend, Rear-Admiral Francis M. Bunce.

In those years of peace George Dewey gained many friends and admirers by his evident ability, his modest firmness of character, his kindly courtesy, and his wide range of interest. In one respect he resembles General Grant. A brother officer says of him: "I have known him fairly well for twenty years, and I have never heard him swear or brag."

CHAPTER XI.

THE BATTLE OF MANILA.

THREE centuries ago the power of Spain in the western hemisphere covered a larger area than the foreign possessions of any other country in Europe. And in the same year in which Cortes, by a romantic and amazing military exploit, brought her the kingdom of Mexico, Magellan discovered for her another rich empire in the Pacific, which she governed, robbed, and oppressed for three hundred and seventy-seven years, until she lost it—probably forever—one May morning, when an American fleet sailed into the bay of Manila and won a victory as complete and astonishing as that of Cortes. The greater part of the reasons why such a victory was possible are indicated in the foregoing pages, but the circumstances that gave occasion for it need explanation.

Spain's misrule in her colonies finally produced in most of them a chronic state of insurrection, and one after another they slipped from her grasp. Peru, Bolivia, Colombia, the Argentine, Mexico, Louisiana, Florida, and the greater part of the West Indies once

Diagram of Manila Bay.

were hers. She ceded Louisiana to France in 1800, and Florida to the United States in 1819, and two years later Mexico achieved her independence. She still had the rich islands of Cuba and Porto Rico in the West Indies, and the Philippine group in the East.

Though there have been revolutions and counter revolutions in Spain since the beginning of this century, the colonies have profited by none of them. Whether the home government was republic or monarchy, it was equally impressed with the idea that colonies were for plunder only. In 1848 the United States offered to buy Cuba for one hundred million dollars, but the offer was indignantly rejected with the remark that there was not gold enough in the world to buy that island from Spain. Of the many insurrections there, the most serious were that which lasted from 1868 to 1878, costing Spain a hundred thousand lives and Cuba nearly sixty thousand, and that which broke out in 1895. In the former of these, forty thousand prisoners who were captured by the Spanish troops were deliberately put to death; and in the latter such barbarous measures of repression were resorted to as subjected, not men alone, but women and children, to the most cruel suffering. Meanwhile, the United States Government was doing its utmost to enforce the laws of neutrality, and a part of its navy was kept busy watching the coasts and thwarting filibustering schemes, some of which were successful in spite of them.

The feelings of horror excited among the American people by the atrocities of the Spanish commander in Cuba began to demand that somehow or other an end be put to them; and every comment on the great powers of Europe for permitting the massacre of Armenians by the Turks, suggested a parallel criticism in regard to the United States and Cuba.

A similar insurrection was in progress in the Philippine Islands. That group is about two hundred miles from the coast of China. The largest of them, Luzon, is about as large as the State of Ohio, and the next, Mindanao, is almost as large; while the smallest are mere islets. There are nearly two thousand in all. The total area is estimated at one hundred and fourteen thousand square miles (about equal to the combined areas of New York, New Jersey, Pennsylvania and Maryland), and the total population at seven million (about equal to that of the State of New York). Of this population more than half are on the island of Luzon. Here also is the capital city, Manila, with a population (including suburbs) of a quarter of a million.

Some of the original tribes remain in the islands, but the present inhabitants are largely Malay, with about ten thousand Spaniards and a good many

Chinese. The principal exports were hemp, sugar, rice, coffee, cocoa, and tobacco. The annual revenue before the war was about fourteen million dollars.

The capital is in latitude fifteen degrees north, about the same as that of Porto Rico, and the southern point of Mindanao is within five degrees of the equator. The group has a length, north and south, of twelve hundred miles. The capital city contained a cathedral, a university, and a palace for the governor. It is on a beautiful land-locked harbor, twenty-six miles from the entrance. This entrance is twelve miles wide, but it is divided by two islands, giving one channel two miles wide and another five miles. The city is divided by the River Pasig, the old town being on the south side, and the new town on the north. The principal fortifications were at Cavité, on a promontory seven miles south of the city, but there were others on Corregidor Island, at the entrance.

In the autumn of 1897 Commodore Dewey's health was impaired—possibly from indoor service—and he was advised to apply for sea duty to restore it. Various accounts are given of his next assignment, not all of which can be true, but on the last day of November he was made commander of the Asiatic squadron, and a month later he hoisted his flag on the Olympia at Nagasaki, Japan.

The growing feeling in the United States of horror and indignation at the state of affairs in Cuba and the Philippines found free expression; this roused the resentment of the Spanish Government and people, and it became evident that not much was required to bring on a war between the two nations. An occurrence most deplorable—whether caused by accident or by design—in the harbor of Havana, in the night of February 14, 1898, brought on the crisis. This was the blowing up of the United States battle ship Maine by a submarine mine or torpedo. The vessel was completely wrecked, and two hundred and sixty-six lives were destroyed. She was riding at anchor, on the spot selected for her by the Spanish harbor authorities, and the greater part of the crew were asleep in their hammocks. Probably nine tenths of the American people believed that the ship had been blown up by treachery, but the moderation and forbearance of both people and Government, while they waited for the result of an official investigation, were remarkable. The Court of Inquiry was composed of experienced officers of high rank, who sat twenty-three days and employed divers and experts. Their unanimous verdict, delivered on March 21st, declared that "the ship was destroyed by the explosion of a submarine mine, which caused the partial explosion of two or more of her forward magazines, and no evidence has been obtainable fixing the responsibility for the destruction of the Maine upon any person or persons." If it was proved that the wreck was the work of a submarine mine, it was not difficult to guess where the responsibility lay. Congress boldly attributed the disaster to "the crime or the criminal negligence of the Spanish officials," and the people generally agreed with Congress on this point.

Several members of Congress, notably Senator Proctor, formerly Secretary of War, visited Cuba to see the condition of affairs for themselves; and their reports, with the sickening details, increased the determination of the American people to interfere in the cause of humanity.

On March 9th, at the President's request, Congress passed unanimously a bill appropriating fifty million dollars as an emergency fund to be used for the national defense.

In a special message, April 11th, the President recited the facts, and said: "The forcible intervention of the United States as a neutral to stop the war, according to the large dictates of humanity, and following many historical precedents where neighboring states have interfered to check the hopeless sacrifice of life by internecine conflicts beyond their borders, is justifiable on rational grounds." Eight days later Congress passed a joint resolution declaring war. This date, April 19th, was the anniversary of the first bloodshed in the American Revolution (1775), and also of the first in the civil war (1861). Measures for increasing both the army and the navy had been taken already.

The United States naval squadron at Hong Kong included most of our force in the Pacific and was well supplied; and the cruiser Baltimore, with a large quantity of stores and ammunition, was added. It now consisted of four protected cruisers—the Olympia, the Baltimore, the Boston, and the Raleigh—from 3,000 to 5,870 tons each, and the gunboats Concord and Petrel. It carried in all one hundred and thirty-three guns. Its commander, George Dewey, was of the same age as Farragut at the beginning of the civil war—sixty.

The Commodore had received provisional orders, instructing him, in case of war with Spain, to capture or destroy the Spanish fleet in the Pacific and take possession of the Philippine Islands; and he was now promptly notified that he might carry them out. The British authorities at Hong Kong gave notice that the fleet must leave that port at once, in accordance with the laws of neutrality, and on April 27th Dewey sailed for the Chinese port in Mirs Bay, and there completed his preparations. One day later, having given the American consul time to get away from Manila, he sailed for Subig Bay, thirty miles north of that city, expecting to find the Spanish fleet there; but it had just gone to Manila Bay, where it could have the protection of shore batteries.

This fleet was commanded by Admiral Montojo. Its fighting vessels were seven cruisers—the Reina Maria Cristina, the Castilla, the Velasco, the Don Antonio de Ulloa, the Don Juan de Austria, the Isla de Cuba, and the Isla de Luzon—the gunboats El Cano and General Lezo, and four torpedo boats. The size of the cruisers was from 1,030 to 3,520 tons, and the whole number of guns carried was one hundred and thirteen.

Some of the Spanish officials cherished certain delusions that appear to have originated with the Spanish newspapers. One was, that if the United States Government engaged in a foreign war the Southern States would again secede. Another was, that the United States navy was without discipline and without competent officers, and that the crews were the mere riffraff of all nations, attracted thither by the liberal pay. The Governor-General of the Philippines issued a boastful proclamation in which he set forth these ideas, and added (more truthfully, perhaps, than he suspected), "The struggle will be short and decisive."

Whether justly or not, there were suspicions of the genuineness of the neutrality to be observed by other powers, and an incident at Hong Kong showed that Commodore Dewey was not to be trifled with in the discharge of his duty. The German Emperor's brother, Prince Henry, called on Dewey in the flagship, and said in the course of the conversation, "I will send my ships to Manila, to see that you behave." "I shall be delighted to have your Highness do so," Dewey answered, "but permit me to caution you to keep your ships from between my guns and the enemy."

The American fleet followed the Spanish fleet to Manila Bay without loss of time, and early Sunday morning, May 1st, the Spaniards were astonished to see their enemy sailing in through the south channel. When half the squadron had passed in, one of the land batteries opened fire, but without effect. The ships continued at slow speed across the great bay, looking for their antagonists, and found them in a smaller bay—known as Baker Bay—anchored in line across its entrance, their left and right protected by batteries on the inclosing peninsula and on the mainland. Two mines were exploded ahead of the American flagship as it advanced, but produced no damage. When the fleets were nearly parallel with each other, the distance being two thousand to five thousand yards, the Commodore said to the captain of the Olympia: "You may fire when you are ready, Gridley," and at once the battle began. Then was seen the advantage of training and target practice to the men behind the guns. The American fire was remarkable for its precision, and almost every shot told, while the Spanish fire, though vigorous, was ineffective. The Spanish flagship attempted to leave the line and go out to engage the Olympia at close range, but at once the entire battery of the Olympia was concentrated on her, and she retreated to her former place.

Following the example set by Du Pont at Hilton Head in 1861, the fleet steamed steadily by and returned in a long ellipse, firing the starboard broadsides as they went up, and the port broadsides as they came back. This was repeated five times. The land batteries near the city, as well as those on Cavité point, opened fire on the fleet, but the Americans did not reply to them, their first business being with the Spanish vessels. Dewey sent word to the Governor-General that unless the city batteries ceased the city would be shelled, and this had the desired effect. The terrific assault crippled the Spanish vessels, set two of them on fire, and killed a great many men; but the Spanish sailors were not so deficient in courage as in skill, and they stood by their guns manfully.

Admiral Montojo says in his report: "The enemy shortened the distance between us, and, rectifying his aim, covered us with a rain of rapid-fire projectiles. At half past seven one shell completely destroyed the steering-gear. I ordered to steer by hand while the rudder was out of action. In the meanwhile another shell exploded on the poop and put nine men out of action. Another carried away the mizzen masthead, bringing down the flag and my ensign, which were replaced immediately. A fresh shell exploded in the officers' cabin, covering the hospital with blood and destroying the wounded who were being treated there. Another exploded in the ammunition room astern, filling the quarters with smoke and preventing the working of the hand steering-gear. As it was impossible to control the fire, I had to flood the magazine when the cartridges were beginning to explode. Amidships several shells of smaller caliber went through the smokestack, and one of the large ones penetrated the fire room, putting out of action one master gunner and twelve men serving the guns. Another rendered useless the starboard bow gun. While the fire astern increased, fire was started forward by another shell which went through the hull and exploded on the deck. The broadside guns, being undamaged, continued firing until only one gunner and one seaman remained unhurt for working them, as the guns' crews had been frequently called upon to substitute those charged with steering, all of whom were out of action. The ship being out of control, . . . I gave the order to sink and abandon her before the magazines should explode."

Isle de Cuba. Isle de Luzon. Rena Cristoa. Cavite Batteries. Boston. Baltimore. Raleigh. Olympia. Concord

The battle of Manila.

(By the courtesy of F. A. Munsey.)

All this was on the flagship, and the other Spanish vessels had been used only a little less roughly when the American fleet drew off to rest the men and have breakfast. How much the rest and refreshment were needed can be realized only by those who themselves have been at work in "the iron dens and caves" while the battle was raging overhead. A stoker on the Olympia, giving an account of his experiences during the fight, said: "The battle hatches were all battened down, and we were shut in this little hole, the ventilating pipes being the only things left open. The temperature was nearly up to two hundred degrees, and it was so hot our hair was singed. There were several leaks in the steam pipes, and the hissing steam made things worse. The clatter of the engines and the roar of the furnaces made such a din it seemed one's head would burst. When a man could stand it no longer he would put his head under the air pipe for a moment. We could tell when our guns opened fire by the way the ship shook. Once in a while one of the apprentice boys would come to our ventilating pipe and shout down to tell us what was going on."

Soon after eleven o'clock the American fleet returned to the attack, and at this time the Spaniard's flagship and most of his other vessels were in flames. At half past twelve the firing ceased, for the task was substantially completed; one after another the hostile ships had been sunk or driven ashore and burned, and the Americans had also poured such a fire into the batteries at Cavité as compelled their surrender. Dewey's fleet then anchored near the city, leaving the gunboat Petrel to complete the destruction of the smaller Spanish boats that remained, which was done.

Thus in about four hours of fighting the American had annihilated the Spanish power in the Pacific and won a new empire. Admiral Montojo reported his losses as three hundred and eighty-one men killed or wounded. In the American fleet seven men were slightly wounded, but none were killed. Some of the ships were struck by the Spanish shot, but not one was seriously injured.

A pretty anecdote is told of Dewey after the battle. When the order had been given to strip for action a powder boy lost his coat overboard. He asked permission to go for it, but was refused. He went to the other side of the ship, went over, and recovered his coat, and was then placed under arrest for disobedience; and after the battle he was tried and found guilty. When the sentence was submitted to the Commodore he was curious to know why any one should risk his life for a coat, and asked the boy. The little fellow, after some hesitation, told him it was because his mother's picture was in the pocket. The tears came to Dewey's eyes as he gave orders for his release, saying, "A boy that loves his mother enough to risk his life for her picture can not be kept in irons on this fleet."

While no American had any doubt of the result of a war with Spain, the whole world was astonished at a battle that had completely destroyed one fleet without serious damage to the other. It was evident that a people who had produced John Paul Jones, Hull, Porter, Stewart, Bainbridge, Perry, Decatur, Farragut, Worden, and Winslow had not yet lost the power of producing worthy successors to those naval heroes.

If one wishes to muse on the historic achievements of sea power, it is not necessary to visit Copenhagen or the Nile, or sit on the shore of Trafalgar Bay; the Mississippi and Manila Bay will answer quite as well. The United States navy has often been criticised at home and sneered at abroad; but it is notable that in every war in which it has engaged it has surpassed all expectations; and there is no reason to suppose it will not continue to do so as long as the nation endures.

> "When life's last sun gaes feebly down,
>   And death comes to their door,
> When a' the world's a dream to them,
>   They'll go to sea no more."

CHAPTER XII.

AFTER THE BATTLE.

The first reports of the victory in Manila Bay were received with amazement and with considerable incredulity. Among Americans there was little doubt —perhaps none at all—as to the result of the war; but they did not think to get through it without considerable losses, and they expected the heaviest ones to fall on the navy. The reason for this was in the new and untried character of naval architecture and armament. From the sailing vessels that fought the famous battles of 1812 to the steamers with which Farragut passed the batteries on the Mississippi the change was not so great and radical as from these to the fleet commanded by Dewey. The cruiser of to-day, with its massive sides of metal, its heavy rifled guns with improved projectiles, its rapid fire, its electric lights and signals, its search-lights and range-finders, and other apparatus contributing to celerity and accuracy of work, is more dangerous and destructive, so long as it remains intact, than anything that Hull or Bainbridge, Du Pont or Farragut, ever saw. But it is

Admiral Dewey on the bridge of the Olympia.
(By the courtesy of the Judge Company.)

a complicated machine, and nobody knew what it would do if seriously crippled, the probability being that it would go to the bottom and leave not a floating plank to which any poor sailor could cling. At the same time a great deal of money and ingenuity had been spent in building torpedo boats—more by European governments than by ours—and it was apprehended that these at sea would be like the proverbial snake in the grass on land—able to dart quickly and inflict a mortal wound on greater and nobler creations than themselves. And then came the construction of the still swifter craft known as torpedo-boat destroyers, with appalling stories of their deadly nature. And with all these complex forces afloat there was a very natural dread of seeing them tried in actual battle, for it was feared that even the victor could not attain his victory without fearful disaster.

So when the news was confirmed that an American fleet, paying no heed to the probability of torpedoes in the channel, had steamed into Manila Bay by night and in a few hours had sunk or destroyed a fleet of nearly equal rating, and then had silenced and captured powerful land batteries—and this without the loss of a ship or a man—" all the world wondered," not merely in the imagination of a poet describing a useless exploit, but in reality, because it recognized a marvelous revolution in the art of war. History recorded no such victory until this was repeated in Cuban waters, two months later, by another American fleet. Nelson had destroyed the fleets of England's enemies, but not without blood on the English decks and sorrow in English homes. He lost nearly nine hundred men in the battle of the Nile, nearly a thousand in the battle of the Baltic, and more than fifteen hundred at Trafalgar.

Throughout the United States there was pride and rejoicing, and Dewey became a household word. It appeared everywhere, and was given as an honored name to all sorts of things, from a popgun or a terrier to a park or a theatre. In Europe the student of history could hardly help putting together four facts and suspecting the existence of some significant condition or principle behind them—that American naval vessels had demonstrated their superiority over the English in 1812; that it was an American fleet that, a little later, put an end to the payment of tribute by civilized nations to the Algerine pirates; that the Monitor, an American invention, had revolutionized warfare by water in 1862; and that American cruisers and gunboats had now had it all their own way in spite of Spanish cruisers, submarine mines, forts, and torpedo boats. European governments were anxious to know how it was done, and their military authorities dispatched officers across the Atlantic to find out. The general explanation was the superiority of the men behind the guns, with their abundant training and perfect discipline. The particular reasons for the result were given by Admiral Dewey in conversation with a friend. He said:

"The battle of Manila Bay was fought in Hong Kong Harbor—that is, the hard work was done there; the execution here was not difficult. With the co-operation of the officers of the fleet, my plans were carefully studied out there, and no detail was omitted. Any man who had a suggestion to offer was heard, and if it was a good one it was adopted. After the indications of war were so strong that it appeared inevitable, I devoted my time and energies to making every preparation possible. When we left Hong Kong and anchored in Mirs Bay, outside of the neutrality limits, I had determined upon my line of action. When we left there a few days later we sailed away ready for battle, and expecting it as soon as we reached the neighborhood of Manila.

"From that hour of departure until we drew out of action, Sunday morning, May 1st, after destroying the Spanish squadron, we practically did not stop the engines of our ships. We came directly across from the China port to that of Luzon, headed down toward the entrance of Manila Bay, reconnoitred Subig Bay, where it had been rumored we would find the enemy, made the entrance to Manila, passed Corregidor Island by the south channel in the darkness of the night, and steamed across the bay close to Manila, where at break of day we discovered the Spanish fleet off Cavité. Signaling to prepare for action and follow the flagship, I gave orders to steam past the enemy and engage their ships. The result you can see by looking at the sunken vessels in the harbor.

"Every ship and every man did his duty well, and the marvel of it all is, that not one man on our side was killed or even seriously injured. The only harm inflicted on the ships was of a trivial nature, although the Spaniards kept up a lively fire until their gun decks were no longer out of water or they had no men to man the guns. The Spanish admiral and officers and crew fought bravely, and deserve credit for their valor."

In giving his views of the action, he said:

"The first lesson of the battle teaches the importance of American gunnery and good guns. It confirms my early experiences under Admiral Farragut, that combats are decided more by skill in gunnery and the quality of the guns than by all else. Torpedoes and other appliances are good in their way, but are of secondary importance. The Spaniards, with their combined fleet and forts, were equal to us in gun power, but they were unable to harm us because of bad gunnery. Constant practice had made our gunnery destructive, and won the victory.

"The second lesson of this battle is the complete demonstration of the value of high-grade men. Cheap men are not wanted, are not needed, are a loss to the United States navy. We should have none but the very best men behind the guns. It will not do to have able officers and poor men. The men in their class must be the equal of the officers in theirs. We must have the best men filling all the posts on shipboard. To make the attainments of the officers valuable, we must have, as we have in this fleet, the best men to carry out their commands.

"The third lesson, not less important than the others, is the necessity for inspection. Everything to be used in a battle should have been thoroughly inspected by naval officials. If this is done, there will be no failure at a crisis in time of danger. Look at the difference between our ships and the Spanish ships. Everything the Spaniards had was supplied by contract. Their shells, their powder, all their materials were practically worthless, while ours were perfect."

While the engagement was in progress every place in Manila that commanded a view of the bay was crowded with spectators. There is a curious mingling of simplicity and pathos in the comments of a Spanish newspaper published in Manila. It said: "Who could have imagined that they would have the rashness stealthily to approach our shores, provoking our defenders to an unavailing display of skill and valor, in which, alas! balls could not be propelled by heart throbs, else the result would have been different? The sound of the shots from our batteries and those from the enemy's ships, which awakened the citizens of Manila at five o'clock on that May morning, transformed the character of our peaceful and happy surroundings. Frightened at the prospect of dangers that seemed greater than they were, women and children in carriages, or by whatever means they could, sought refuge in the outskirts of the city, while all the men, from the highest to the lowest, the merchant and the mechanic, the soldier and the peasant, the dwellers in the interior and those of the coast, repaired to their posts and took up arms, confident that never, except by passing over their dead bodies, should the soil of Manila be defiled by the enemy, notwithstanding that from the first it was apparent that the armored ships and powerful guns were invulnerable to any effort at our command. . . . A soldier of the first battalion of sharpshooters, who saw the squadron so far out of range of our batteries, said, glancing up to heaven, 'If the Holy Mary would only transform that water into land, then the Yankees would see how we could fight.' And a Malay who was squatting near by exclaimed, 'Let them land, and we will crush them under heel.'"

The relative power of the opposing fleets may be seen from this summary: The Americans had four cruisers, two gunboats, and one cutter, carrying fifty-seven classified large guns, seventy-six rapid-firing and machine guns, and one thousand eight hundred and eight men. The Spaniards had seven cruisers, five gunboats, and four torpedo boats, carrying fifty-two classified large guns, eighty-three rapid-firing and machine guns, and one thousand nine hundred and forty-nine men.

Commodore Dewey's fleet officers were: Commander Benjamin P. Lamberton, chief of staff; Lieutenant Thomas M. Brumby, flag lieutenant; Ensign Harry H. Caldwell, secretary.

The line officers of the Olympia were: Captain Charles V. Gridley, Lieutenant-Commander Sumner C. Paine, Lieutenants Corwin P. Rees, Carlos G. Calkins, Valentine S. Nelson, Stokely Morgan, and Samuel M. Strite, and Ensigns Montgomery M. Taylor, Frank B. Upham, William P. Scott, Arthur G. Kavanaugh, and Henry V. Butler.

The line officers of the Baltimore were: Captain Nehemiah M. Dyer, Lieutenant-Commander Gottfried Blockinger, Lieutenants William Braunersreuther, Frank W. Kellogg, John M. Ellicott, and Charles S.

Stanworth, and Ensigns George H. Hayward, Michael J. McCormack, and N. E. Irwin.

The line officers of the Boston were: Captain Frank Wildes, Lieutenant-Commander John A. Norris, Lieutenants John Gibson and William L. Howard, and Ensigns Samuel S. Robinson, Lay H. Everhart, and John S. Doddridge.

The line officers of the Raleigh were: Captain Joseph B. Coghlan, Lieutenant-Commander Frederic Singer, Lieutenants William Winder, Benjamin Tappan, Hugh Rodman, and Casey B. Morgan, and Ensigns Frank L. Chadwick and Provoost Babin.

The line officers of the Concord were: Commander Asa Walker, Lieutenant-Commander George P. Colvocoresses, Lieutenants Thomas B. Howard and Patrick W. Hourigan, and Ensigns Louis A. Kaiser, William C. Davidson, and Orlo S. Knepper.

The line officers of the Petrel were: Commander Edward P. Wood, Lieutenants Edward M. Hughes, Bradley A. Fiske, Albert N. Wood, and Charles P. Plunkett, and Ensigns George L. Fermier and William S. Montgomery.

The cutter McCulloch was commanded by Captain Daniel B. Hodgsdon.

CHAPTER XIII.

THE PROBLEM ON LAND.

AFTER the Spanish fleet had been destroyed and the forts surrendered, Admiral Dewey demanded the surrender of the city of Manila with all its fortifications and military stores. This the Governor-General refused. The fleet could have bombarded the citadel and the fortifications, but as no land force was at hand to garrison the place, and the foreign consuls advised against it from fear of revengeful action of the insurgents, the Admiral refrained. Instead, he established a strict blockade of the port, while the Filipinos were besieging the city on the land side. He destroyed six batteries at the entrance of the bay, and occupied Cavité, where he established hospitals in which the sick and wounded Spaniards were protected and cared for. As his proposal that both sides use the telegraph cable unmolested was not accepted by the Governor-General, he had it lifted and cut.

The possibility of a peaceful settlement of affairs in the island had been destroyed by this same Governor, who in an official proclamation had told the natives that the Americans had murdered all the original inhabitants of North America, and that now they were coming to rob the Filipinos of their lands, reduce many of them to slavery, and substitute the Prostestant religion for the Catholic. And the Archbishop of Manila supplemented this with a pastoral letter in which he told the natives that if the Americans were victorious their altars would be desecrated, their churches turned into Protestant chapels, vice inculcated instead of morality, and every effort made to lead their children away from the true faith.

While affairs on shore were thus working toward a serious condition of things for all concerned, there had been indications of unfriendliness and a disposition to embarrass the operations of the Americans by some of the commanders of foreign war ships. This was so marked on the part of the Germans that there was serious danger of a rupture of the friendly relations between the two countries; but the tact and firmness of Dewey, who had been intrusted with full discretion by his Government, prevented it. None the less anxiously he looked for the arrival from the United States of a sufficient land force to capture and hold Manila, and he was obliged to use all his skill in diplomacy to restrain the Filipinos from attacking the city.

As soon as an expedition could be prepared, the Government sent one, in three divisions. The first, under General Francis V. Greene, sailed from San Francisco May 25th, and arrived at Manila June 30th; the second, under General Thomas H. Anderson, sailed June 3d; and the third, under General Arthur McArthur, arrived July 31st. The whole number of troops was nearly twelve thousand. With the third section went General Wesley Merritt, commander of the expedition, who also had been appointed Military Governor of the Philippines; and with him went General Elwell S. Otis, to whom was given the command of all the troops in the Philippines, leaving General Merritt free to give his energies to the administrative and political problems. On the 4th of August the fleet was strengthened by the arrival of the monitor Monterey, which had heavier ordnance than the ten-inch Krupp guns that the Spaniards had mounted in the shore batteries.

The troops were landed at Cavité, and occupied the trenches on the south side of the city, while the Filipino insurgents held those on the east and north. The Spanish Governor-General resigned his authority to the military commander, and, with the permission of Admiral Dewey, was taken away on a German cruiser. On the 28th of July the Spaniards made a determined assault on the American lines, but were driven back; and on August 7th Admiral Dewey and General Merritt gave notice that in forty-eight hours they would attack the defenses. Parleying ensued, and the Americans extended the time nearly a week in order that General Merritt might push his lines farther east and take possession of the bridges, and thus be able to prevent the insurgents from entering the city to loot it and massacre the Spaniards, which they were bent upon doing. On the morning of August 13th the fleet bombarded the fortifications of Malaté, setting fire to the stores and ammunition, while the Utah battery played on the breastworks. Then the Colorado regiment and the California troops stormed the works, drove out the Spaniards, and fought them from house to house till they reached the esplanade, when a white flag was displayed and the Spanish commander surrendered and was accorded the honors of war. Bodies of insurgents were found entering the city, and were driven back by General Greene's troops.

General Merritt issued a proclamation in which he assured the inhabitants of the islands that he had only come to protect them in their homes, their occupations, and their personal and religious rights; that the port of Manila would be open to the merchant ships of all neutral nations; and that no person would be disturbed so long as he preserved the peace. Additional troops were sent out, and General Merritt returned home, leaving General Otis in command.

Meanwhile, the Spanish fleet on the coast of Cuba had been destroyed, July 3d, by an American fleet under Acting Rear-Admiral William T. Sampson, with Commodore Winfield S. Schley second in command; the defenses of Santiago had been captured by the land forces under General William R. Shafter; the island of Porto Rico was crossed and occupied by an expedition under General Nelson A. Miles; and the French Ambassador at Washington, in behalf of the Spanish Government, had opened negotiations for peace. He and Secretary of State William R. Day signed a protocol on August 12th. This provided for a cessation of hostilities; that Spain should relinquish all claim to Cuba, and cede Porto Rico to the United States; that the American forces should hold the city and bay of Manila pending the conclusion of a treaty of peace, which should determine what would be done with the Philippines; and that peace commissioners should be appointed by both governments, to meet in Paris not later than October 1, 1898. The commissioners on the part of the United States were Secretary Day, Senator Cushman K. Davis, Senator William P. Frye, Hon. Whitelaw Reid, and Senator George Gray. The treaty of peace, as finally agreed to, November 28th, gave the Philippines to the United States, with the stipulation that the American Government should pay twenty million dollars to Spain for her betterments in those islands. This treaty was promptly signed by President McKinley, and after much delay was ratified by the Senate, in spite of a determined attempt to defeat it. The opponents based their objections mainly on what they considered the bad policy and dishonesty of retaining the Philippines.

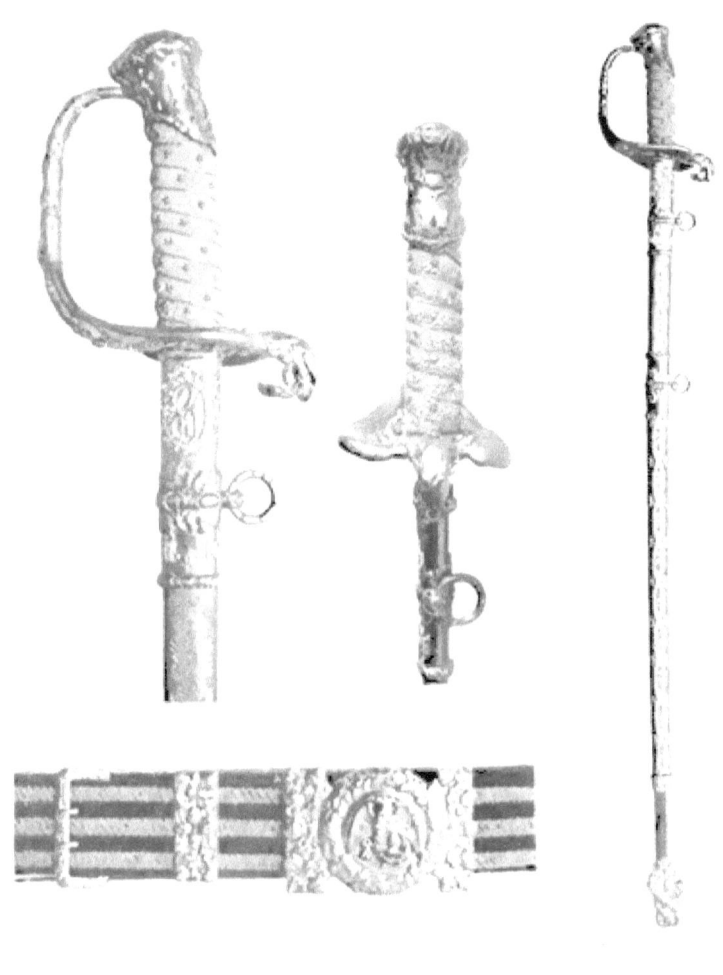

The Dewey Sword, the gift of the nation to Admiral Dewey.
(Tiffany & Co., New York, makers.)

CHAPTER XIV.

HONORS.

Dewey's dispatches of May 1st and 4th, announcing the naval victory and the capture of Cavité, were as brief and modest as possible. The shower of honors that immediately fell upon him was such as perhaps no other man has received within the memory of this generation. The Secretary of the Navy, John D. Long, telegraphed to him, under date of May 7th: "The President, in the name of the American people, thanks you and your officers and men for your splendid achievement and overwhelming victory. In recognition he has appointed you Acting Admiral, and will recommend a vote of thanks to you by Congress."

Two days later the President sent a special message to Congress, in which, after briefly recounting the victory, he said: "Outweighing any material advantage is the moral effect of this initial success. At this unsurpassed achievement the great heart of our nation throbs, not with boasting nor with greed of conquest, but with deep gratitude that this triumph has come in a just cause, and that by the grace of God an effective step has thus been taken toward the attainment of the wished-for peace. To those whose skill, courage, and devotion have won the fight, to the gallant commander and the brave officers and men who aided him, our country owes an incalculable debt. Feeling as our people feel, and speaking in their name, I sent a message to Commodore Dewey, thanking him and his officers and men for their splendid achievement, and informing him that I had appointed him an Acting Rear Admiral. I now recommend that, following our national precedents, and expressing the fervent gratitude of every patriotic heart, the thanks of Congress be given Acting Rear-Admiral George Dewey, of the United States navy, for highly distinguished conduct in conflict with the enemy, and to the officers and men under his command for their gallantry in the destruction of the enemy's fleet and the capture of the enemy's fortifications in the bay of Manila."

Congress promptly, enthusiastically, and unanimously, by a rising vote, passed the joint resolution of thanks to Admiral Dewey and to the officers and men of his fleet.

Then a bill was passed unanimously increasing the number of rear admirals from six to seven, and the President at once promoted Dewey to the full rank.

Furthermore, a resolution was passed unanimously instructing the Secretary of the Navy to present a sword of honor to Admiral Dewey, and cause bronze medals to be struck commemorating the battle of Manila Bay, and distribute them to the officers and men who had participated in the battle, and the sum of ten thousand dollars was appropriated for the purpose.

Two days before the adjournment, in March, 1899, Congress passed, without division, a bill reviving the grade and rank of Admiral in the United States navy, " to provide prompt and adequate reward to Rear-Admiral George Dewey, the said grade and rank to exist only during the lifetime of this officer." The President signed the bill and gave Admiral Dewey the commission on the 2d of March. This made him the ranking officer not only of the navy, but of the army as well, in any operations where the two arms of the service are employed.

Montpelier celebrated the victory with a public demonstration on the 9th of May, in which ten thousand persons participated.

The legislatures of several States passed complimentary resolutions, and in Pennsylvania and California May 1st was made a legal holiday in commemoration of the victory.

Money was raised by private subscription for a

statue of Admiral Dewey, to be cut in Vermont marble and placed beside that of Ethan Allen in the State House at Montpelier. Many colleges conferred honorary degrees upon him, and learned societies and social organizations elected him to honorary membership.

It is proposed to erect a beautiful memorial hall, as an addition to the buildings of Norwich Academy, and name it Dewey Hall.

When, in the summer of 1899, he was relieved and ordered home, he came slowly, stopping often for rest on shore and being everywhere received with honor. A great reception, with an immense procession and other demonstrations, was prepared for him in the city of New York, where he was to arrive on the 28th of September.

Bronze tablet for forward turret of Admiral Dewey's flagship, Olympia.

Presented by citizens of Olympia, Wash.

CHAPTER XV.

LETTERS.

WHEN a man has become famous, there is at once a desire on the part of the public to know something of his character and habits of thought aside from the work that has brought him into notice, and these are generally shown best by his letters. We are permitted to make a few significant extracts from Admiral Dewey's correspondence, with which we will close this volume.

Several Confederate veterans at Clarksville, Tenn., some of whom had belonged to the battery that destroyed the Mississippi when she was trying to pass Port Hudson, sent him a letter of congratulation. In his reply, dated July 23, 1898, he said: "I can assure you that, although I have had letters, resolutions, telegrams, etc., from all parts of the United States, none has given me more pleasure than the communication from you. One fortunate result of this war with Spain is the healing of all the wounds that have been rankling since 1865, and I believe that from now on we will be a united people, with no North, no South. That result alone will be worth all the sacrifices we have made. It would give me much pleasure to talk over with you those stirring days around Port Hudson, and I hope that pleasure may be in store for me."

Under date of October 3, 1898, he wrote to Mrs. Noss, of Mount Pleasant, Penn., whose husband had been killed in the battle of Maleté: "I wish to express to you my deepest sympathy. It must lessen your sorrow somewhat to know that your young husband fell fighting bravely for his country, the noblest death a man can know. From the Olympia I watched the fight that fearful night, and wondered how many American homes would be saddened by the martyrdom suffered by our brave men, and my sympathy went out to each and every one of them. Your loss has been sadder than the others, and I am unable to express the sorrow I feel for you. Tears came to my eyes as I read the sad story of the father who never saw his child, and then the loss of all that was left to the brave mother. It is hard sometimes to believe, but our Heavenly Father, in his infinite goodness, always does things for the best, and some day father, mother, and daughter will be joined, never again to be parted. With my tenderest sympathy, believe me your sincere friend."

In a letter to a friend he wrote, after briefly describing the battle: "The Spanish Admiral Montojo fought his ships like a hero. He stood on his quarter-deck until his ship was ablaze from stem to stern, and

The Dewey Triumphal Arch in Madison Square, New York.

(From the model, by the courtesy of the designer, Charles R. Lamb.)

absolutely sinking under his feet; then, transferring his flag to the Isla de Cuba, he fought with what was left of his fleet, standing fearlessly amid a hail of shrapnel until his second ship and over one hundred of her crew sank like lead in a whirl of water. It seems to me that history in its roll of heroes should make mention of an admiral who could fight his ships so bravely and stand on the bridge coolly and calmly when his fleet captain was torn to pieces by one of our shells at his side. I sent him a message telling him how I appreciated the gallantry with which he had fought his ships, and the deep admiration my officers and men felt for the commander of the Reina Cristina, who nailed his colors to his mast and then went down with his gallant crew. I think, my dear Norton, that had you witnessed this, as I did, you too would have sent the brave sailor the message I caused to be sent to him, to which he responded most courteously."

Political parties are fain to seize upon popular heroes for their presidential candidates—often without much reference to the hero's former political affiliations or want of them. The response is not always such an emphatic refusal as was given once by General Sherman, and now by Admiral Dewey. This is what the Admiral said:

"I would not accept a nomination for the presidency of the United States. I have no desire for any political office. I am unfitted for it, having neither the education nor the training. I am deeply grateful for many expressions of kindly sentiment from the American people, but I desire to retire in peace to the enjoyment of my old age. The navy is one profession, politics is another. I am too old to learn a new profession now. I have no political associations, and my health would never stand the strain of a canvass. I have been approached by politicians repeatedly, in one way or another, but I have refused absolutely to consider any proposition whatever. This is final."

THE END.